Never has a book been so eloquently written and expressed that you forget you are reading. Once you allow yourself to be drawn into the divine cosmos that Hal describes, you will become absorbed in the sweetness of remembrance his words will bring to you. The essays are not unlike the songs you would expect to hear from Spirit echoing throughout the universe. You will embrace the homecoming with open arms and experience the peace with an open heart, which will inevitably open our minds to ALL THERE IS.

The cosmic connection is undeniable and becomes more obvious in each chapter. The message is clear and reaches in to grab hold of whatever may be blocking the door to freedom and infinite joy. Hal opens the door with crystal clarity, humility and excitement you can feel on every page. I could not put this down; it was too familiar yet unheard of in our times. Hal is a visionary; he seeks to bring connected awareness to all who dwell here. It is his gift and I am grateful to receive such divine wisdom. How to live an extraordinary life in an ordinary world. How to be what you are and share that essence with all those around you. How to move beyond the conceptions of humanity and into the realms of infinite consciousness.

Reverend Cherise Thorne, Author of Knowing Spirit and Blessings of Liberation, Co-Founder of the Temple of the Knowing Spirit. (www.knowingspirit.org)

To TRACI —

LiFE is For The ExPerience.

Thanks For Sharing Part
oF Yours With mE!

Love,

7/26/08

SHORT SLEEVES INSIGHTS:

LIVE AN ORDINARY LIFE IN A NON-ORDINARY WAY

BY HAL MANOGUE

Copyright™

TM

Dedication
To my parents Peggy and Ham

Each Other

In Gratitude
We Become
The Giver
And
The Receiver

In Love
We Become
The Gift

In Beauty
We Become
Diverse

In Truth
We Become
Whole

In Light
We Become
One

In Life
We Become
Each Other

Hal Manogue, from the 2008 Collection of
Short Sleeves A Book for Friends

Special Thanks

Yvonne Perry: My friend and writing star who helped make this book a reality. **www.writersinthesky.com**

Kathleen Jacoby: My friend and avid supporter who is my inspiration and guiding light. **www.visionofthegrail.com**

Janet Grace Riehl: My friend and confidant who is pure inspiration and energy. **www.riehlife.com**

Cherise Thorne: My friend and spiritual guide who lives in this world and many other worlds of love. **www.knowingspirit.com**

Suzanne Lieurance: My friend and coach who helped make this book possible through her unconditional service. **www. lieurancegroup.com**

Jessica Dockter: My new friend and graphic designer who dressed this book so beautifully! **www.leedesign.org**

Charles "Tom" Brown: My friend and hero.

To my co-authors: All the sages and teachers who shared their thoughts so this work could be written.

To my readers who bring this work into their world of wonder.

Contents

Copyright 2
Special Thanks...4
Contents 5
Author's Note 10
Hal's Facts 12
Moment of Thanks...14
Introduction..15
A Note about the Editor 17
I've Had Secrets! 19
Opening...**21**
  1. All Streams Start Somewhere! 22
  2. A Sense of Matter...24
  3. Stressed Out? 26
  4. A Thousand Years Forgotten 28
  5. A Word about Nothing......................................30
  6. Being is What?...32
  7. I am Living Art...34
  8. Birds Don't Resemble Eggs 37
  9. I Found it by Myself..39
  10. The Truth Is..41
  11. Good Morning...44
  12. Here's to a New Level of Thinking 45
  13. Twilight 47
The Self...**49**
  1. A Heart Full Of Honey 50
  2. A Loftier Race? 52
  3. Am I a Bird or a Worm? 54
  4. A Puddle of Illusions 56
  5. A Spotless Mind 58
  6. Green and Blue Make Turquoise 60
  7. The Snake-Catcher and the Frozen Snake 62
  8. How Am I Marking Time? 65
  9. I've Got To Stop Killing Myself!......................67
  10. I am a Protoplasmal Primordial Atomic Globule! 69
  11. Mirror, Mirror, Is That Me That I See?..........71
  12. Look at Me. I'm the Bee, Butterfly, Brook, and Breeze .73

Movement **75**
   1. An Ocean Sits Within Me 76
   2. Judge Me Not! 78
   3. As I Learn, I Change 80
   4. Are You Ready to Make a Leap? 82
   5. Embraceable Me 84
   6. Everything is Significant 86
   7. Exit and Enter Gracefully 88
   8. Get on the Elephant 90
   9. Earth Rocks 92
   10. Gnats against the Wind 94
   11. Yea, I Am In Awe! 96
   12. Time to Pop the Lid off the Box 98

Growth **101**
   1. A Cinder of Unity 102
   2. A Flowering Universe 104
   3. A Seed of Change 106
   4. A Smile, a Kiss and a Heart Filled with Gratitude 108
   5. A Stage of Fools 110
   6. Circles on Water 112
   7. From My World to Yours 114
   8. Gaps of Silence 116
   9. Girl in Love 118
   10. How's my Garden Grow? 120
   11. Trust Would Settle Every Problem Now 122
   12. Okay, I Accept Myself! 124

Gateway **127**
   1. A Flowing Silence 128
   2. Theory of What? 131
   3. Am I Dreaming Or What? 133
   4. Break Time 135
   5. Day Dream Believer 137
   6. Death by Design? 139
   7. Fuel for Thought 141
   8. Hide And Seek Anyone? 143
   9. I make Footprints! 145
   10. I'm a Little Square 147

11. Unformed or Cooked? 151
12. Where Are My Keys? 153
13. Which Road Is It? 155
Breakthrough **157**
1. You're Welcome 158
2. A Struggle-free Reality 160
3. Comparisons are Odious 162
4. Enlighten What? 164
5. My Trash is Less Trashy! 166
6. Here's To Self-Being 168
7. Here's to the End 170
8. Infinite Play Anyone? 172
9. The Sheltered Life! 173
10. Outrageous? It Doesn't Matter! 175
11. I Dare to Be Myself! 176
12. New Ideas? Or Forgotten Ones? 178
13. Nothing Happened and I Want to Report It! 179
14. What Will it Take To Change? 181
15. Which Way is the Door? 183
Flow **185**
1. A Cling-less Creature 186
2. A Form of Formlessness 188
3. An Island or a Continent? 190
4. Does a Pebble Ever Die? 192
5. Every Now of It 194
6. History Smiles 196
7. Got A Match? 198
8. House Made of Dawn 200
9. Just Let the Creativity Flow 202
10. We Belong To Each Other 204
11. Who is Living Life? 206
12. Silence 207
Joy **209**
1. Am I Really Full of BS? 210
2. Am I Having Fun Yet? 212
3. A Pack Rat of Love 214
4. A Sneerless World 216

5. A Sweat Shop or Magic Shop? 218
6. Boogie to the Bop! 220
7. Come Easy, Go Easy 222
8. Convulsive Respiration 224
9. Did You Hear the One… 226
10. Glowing in Light 228
11. Harmony of Thoughts 230
12. I'm Framed in Space 232
Harvest **235**
1. A Vessel of Freedom 236
2. To be a Tree! 238
3. My Ego Shakes And Wiggles 240
4. The Mouse and the Cheese 242
5. Forever and Ever 244
6. From My Heart and Eyes 246
7. My Offering Is Peace. What's Yours? 248
8. Good Manners Anyone? 250
9. Hope Has Feathers 252
10. Fields Of Buttercups 254
11. Love Diet 256
12. With Each Breath 258
Journey **261**
1. A Choice of Consciousness 262
2. A Creature of the Now 264
3. A Dried up Puddle of Problems 265
4. A Puff in My Sky 267
5. I Am the Future 269
6. A Sage or Ordinary Man 271
7. A World of Snores 272
8. Double Vision? How about Quadruple Vision? 274
9. Faster than the Speed of Light 276
10. What is Real? 278
11. The Tooth Fairy and Santa 280
12. The River of Time 282
Wholeness **285**
1. A Child in a Week 286
2. A Little Soul Searching? 288

3. Am I Forgetting Something? 290
4. Am I Young Enough? 292
5. An Eruption of Emotions 295
6. An Untangled Web 297
7. Body Intelligence 299
8. Bridge of Love 302
9. Champagne Anyone? 305
10. I Will Meet You There 307
11. How Sweet the Lilt 309
12. Shadow Clings to Form 311
One More Thought **315**
Acknowledgments **318**
Contact Page **320**
About the Author **321**

Author's Note

This book contains essays that were written in 2007 and posted to my daily blog (**http://halmanogue.blogspot.com/**). I write in the morning, usually beginning before sunrise, in my home office. I have no idea what I am going to write about each day. I begin with a prayer of thanks and ask for inspiration from my source. I check my e-mails and my friend's blog to see what treats they have on their sites. I briefly read the news, eat a breakfast snack and drink a glass of water.

Then I start to write a poem—usually three or four lines that I will use when I work on my poetry collection for the year.

I have been studying various subjects over the last twenty years and have a wonderful collection of books that surround me in my office. Each morning I pick one of them and begin reading. Within fifteen minutes or so, I have material for my blog. Some distant sage or teacher or writer is there with me in my office, offering words of wisdom. I follow my emotions and begin writing. The essays write themselves. I punch the keys to spell the words, but the essence of thought is already there. It unites with the rest of the collection and each one is filled with love from a distant time and place.

This collection expresses the love of life and the glory of living it. Although it was written in 2007, it is not restricted by this time/ space world. All of the thoughts are universal and exist in the consciousness of everyone. The message of unity within me rings out through the pages. The thoughts creating my reality are confirmed in every language, religion, and time period. I co-create my world and choose how to experience it. I express those experiences in my words and actions and I become what I believe.

I have divided the book into eleven sections. There is an ancient symbol before each section that reflects a thought. These symbols come from the Viking era and were used as an oracle to direct the choices made in physical life. The eleven runes chosen from the twenty-five available are positive signs of well-being. This book is all about the power we have within us to create and experience a world of peace, love, abundance, joy and unity.

I appreciate your interest and love.

H.T.M.

Franklin, Tennessee

December 2007

Hal's Facts

I was born in the Golden Year of the Pig. My Chinese friends tell me that's special, although I'm not really sure why. Perhaps the reason is because it only comes every 60 years, and this year happens to be a Golden Pig year based on the Chinese calendar.

I grew up in the small town of Chalfont, in Bucks County, Pennsylvania. I went to grade school in Doylestown, Pennsylvania—the same town Pearl S. Buck, and James A. Michener called home.

I visited Europe, Taiwan, Hong Kong, Bangkok, Hawaii, and the Virgin Islands before the age of thirty.

I have lived in Chicago, New York, Dallas and Nashville. The first twenty summers of my life were spent at the Jersey Shore.

I have worked in Europe, the Orient, South America, Mexico, and Canada.

I eat left-handed, throw and bat right-handed and think in two unique spheres.

My cat is 17 years old.

Who Am I

"I am a spirit having a human experience. I create my reality through my thoughts and beliefs. I am a cluster of consciousness connected to a stream of love. I take responsibility for the choices I make and the dreams I dream. I am energy filled with the source of all energy and I live simultaneous lives. I am here to experience emotions and to feel the wealth of value fulfillment. I express myself multidimensional and am grateful for the opportunity to be human."

Why should I seek?
I am the same as He
His essence speaks through me.
I have been looking for myself!

~Rumi

Moment of Thanks

Maps Of Intentions
Pinpoint An Instant In Time
Changing Realities
Bring The Birth Of God
To A World Of Forgetfulness

Flickering Consciousness
Awakens New Visions Of Purpose
Salvation Sits On An Altar Of Thought
Draped In Robes Of Awareness

Yesterday's Separation
Is Healed With Vivid
Perceptions Of Unity

The Voice Of Connection
Rings Out Through The Ages
Vibrating Tones Reveal
Mysteries Of Life
In Moments Of Thanks

An Ancient Symbol Changes
Into
The Will Of Freedom
The Desire For Peace
And The Gift Of Love
Within Myself

Hal Manogue,
From the upcoming *2009 Collection of Short Sleeves A Book For Friends*

Introduction

Where this book began and where it ends is hard to put in words. The thoughts throughout the book are recorded in linear time, but they describe a world that is void of our perception of time.

I use the term "All There Is" frequently in the book in order to define our source. It is the connecting phrase that unites the concept of oneness in spirit that makes all of us the same, yet diverse, in physical form. It is the force of energy that expands and grows as we realize who we really are.

We are all here to become grander versions of the spirit that is eternally connected to All There Is. All the people who gave me the inspiration to write this book knew that and shared that knowledge freely. The message is simple: we are all connected to an eternal stream of consciousness that is waiting for us to remember that truth. Once the light goes on, our physical life takes on another dimension. We begin to use our intuition and feelings to make choices that affect the quality of our daily experiences. We accept and forgive rather than fight and kill. We reduce anger and judgment down to a four-letter word: love, and we fill our thoughts with it. The energy of our source vibrates in joy and peace, and abundance becomes the rule, not the exception.

The power to connect to this other world is within all of us. Our thoughts create our experiences and we express our beliefs and become what we think.

Reading the words of the great sages in this book will awaken another aspect of your consciousness and I believe you will remember that we all are spirits having a human experience and we do it by living an ordinary life in a non-ordinary way.

H.T.M.
Franklin, Tennessee

A Note about the Editor

The only joy in the world is to begin.

Cesare Pavese was born in 1908 and was an Italian poet and novelist. Italy considers him one of the greatest authors of the twentieth century. His simple statement about beginning is in fact a joyful experience.

When I begin anything, it's always with excitement and joy. I feel the energy of creation around me; it's in my every thought. My impulses vibrate in harmony with my inner self and something magical happens; things begin to manifest in all sorts of wonderful ways. Writing is a good example of that; just starting the process of writing is a magnificent adventure. New worlds open around me, and people begin to enter my life with vibrant energy. The writing becomes a mode of knowing and I am surrounded by love.

Yvonne Perry is an example of this flowing energy. She is an author, business owner and gentle spirit. Her life is dedicated to the service of others; especially writers who are trying to make a living with their words. I first became aware of Yvonne through my wife, who was interviewed by Yvonne for a book she was writing. We never met physically but I read her book, *More Than Meets the Eye*, and found her to be more than I expected. Her insight and dedication to the subject of the afterlife was informative, comprehensive and enlightening.

Somehow I knew we would meet and become friends and that happened sooner than I expected. When I actually started to send my poetry to people in the writing profession, Yvonne was on the top of my list. I had never been published and was a bit nervous about anyone reading what I had written, but I sent Yvonne one of my poems anyway. In my email, I introduced myself to her and told her a little about me, and then asked her to read my work and let me know her thoughts about it. Almost immediately I got her response and in her loving way she thanked me for connecting with her and told me she had just started a newsletter and would include my poem in the next edition. As you can imagine, I was overwhelmed with excitement.

That gesture filled me with the confidence to continue writing and to express myself with gratitude, just the way Yvonne did for me. The joy I felt beginning my friendship with Yvonne was pure motivation. I felt her love and she continues to give that love to everyone she meets. Her newsletter, which is a group of articles from writers around the globe, is now a 20-plus-page work read by thousands. Her new book, *Right to Recover: Winning the Political and Religious Wars over Stem Cell Research in America*, has just been published and it is a work worth reading.

Everything that Yvonne begins is done in joy; everyone Yvonne meets is met with love. Her example has influenced many writers to continue their journey with confidence and faith. One person does make a difference; Yvonne is an angel dressed as a writer and she touches life with the gift of love.

I start my day writing and reading; I usually visit Yvonne's site and she is always promoting the works of others, which is great inspiration for me. The basic act of connection brings so much light and love into my daily experiences. My friend Yvonne is the plug that fits into that socket of love. Her awareness is the light of unity.

You can visit Yvonne's Website, **http://www.yvonneperry.net/** to learn more about this amazing spirit. Thanks Yvonne, for the joy and the example to just begin.

I've Had Secrets!

Socrates said, *"A happy man was well demonized."* As I look back over my life, I have to agree with him.

I am filled with happiness as I write this essay and I have had my share of demons along the way. In fact, I lived in a state of fear for years.

But why? What was I afraid of? I have lived through family losses, job losses, money losses, property losses, relationship losses and self-esteem losses, and here I am writing this as a happy man. The answers didn't come from someone else; they came from within me. We all know Roosevelt's words about fear, but they really didn't register with me until I started to dig within me. I had secrets—lots of secrets—that I kept hidden from myself. I used so much energy trying to hide these events that I blocked myself from seeing the true me. This blocked energy manifested itself in many ways: sickness, addictions, fantasies and low self-worth to name a few. My life was a secret that overshadowed the good that surrounded me.

The psychology books told me I had to face my fears for they are a reality I created from my own beliefs of good and bad, right and wrong—beliefs that were so strong that I was willing to physically destroy myself rather than face these secret demons. My focused consciousness kept me in a state of fear with no weapon other than my thoughts. I had closed off a part of myself, I buried my secrets in fear, and the evil I had created was the cemetery.

I decided I wanted to change. I wanted to feel better. I wanted my emotions back. The time had come for me to find a solution. I wanted a new life.

One sunny Tennessee morning I sat in the garden among all the living things that had no secrets—the trees, plants, birds and insects—and looked around me. I felt their freedom, their honesty, and their wholeness. So, I reached into my coffin of secrets starting with the very first one I buried many years ago and dug it up. There it was right where I remembered it. I gently put my thoughts around it and kissed it and forgave it. That morning I went through several years of my life accepting all I had hidden and forgiving myself for doing so. Like magic, my energy level seemed to explode and a great weight was lifted from my body. I cried; joyful emotion enfolded within me.

There were many days like that day, each one bringing me closer to my happiness, each one reconnecting me to a self that was hidden. I know now that there are no secrets. I can't hide from myself and I certainly can't hide from others.

What I can do is accept myself as a spirit having a human experience in order to be a grander version of who I really am—a soul connected to all life in truth, freedom and Love.

Opening

1. All Streams Start Somewhere!

When a country obtains great power, it becomes like the sea; all streams run downward into it. The more powerful it grows, the greater the need for humility. Humility means trusting my own truth, thus never needing to be defensive. A great nation is like a great man: when he makes a mistake, he realizes it. Having realized it, he admits it. Having admitted it, he corrects it. He considers those who point out his faults as his most benevolent teachers. He thinks of his enemy as the shadow that he himself casts. If a nation is centered in truth, if it nourishes its own people and doesn't meddle in the affairs of others, it will be a light to all nations in the world.

These words were originally written in Chinese over 2,500 years ago. The author Lao-tzu was an ordinary man. Not much is known about him, but his words explain who he was. His message above is a simple one. Truth is much the same way; it finds its path in freedom.

I look around our great nation and see the enormous effects of its power. I see people realizing the mistakes made by the misuse of that power. I see people trying to correct those mistakes and admitting the devastation they have caused. I see people looking at their enemies and seeing themselves in their eyes. I see the opportunity to change my beliefs and listen to my benevolent teachers, who want nothing but truth to be my power. I see the flicker of light that will illuminate the hearts of all nations.

Mistakes are the steps to humility. I walk on those steps and reach out and touch the world with my love and forgiveness. I become the light that shines for all to see. My truth is love. My truth is power. My truth is peace.

Lao-tzu has a simple message for all of us. Look within yourself and find the answers; they are waiting for us to remember them. There is no greater power than truth; it is within all of us. Truth is awareness, connection, and unity. It is abundant and free and it has no opposite.

Remembering who I am—a spirit filled with truth—brings peace and joy to the world.

2. A Sense of Matter

Pierre Teilhard De Chardin was born in 1881. He was a French Jesuit priest, paleontologist, and philosopher. His book, *The Phenomenon of Man*, was a sweeping account of the unfolding of the cosmos. The church was displeased with his work, so none of his works were published in his lifetime. Pope John XXIII rehabilitated him posthumously and his writings have been considered an important influence on the church's stance on evolution.

I found some of Pierre's work this morning and it gave me a distinct awareness of matter. All the matter around me is special. The universe and all the matter in it is there for me to learn and grow from. It is something to bless and Pierre's words do it beautifully.

Louis Nizer, the twentieth century lawyer and author said, *"True religion is the life we lead, not the creed we profess."* Pierre's church religion turned its back on him, only to find his life's religion to be an important tool in its quest for remembering. I am sharing his work this morning with pleasure, and with the understanding that I am connected to all matter and it is there for me to appreciate and accept with gratitude.

Blessed be you, harsh matter, barren soil, stubborn rock, you who yield only to force, you who cause us to work if we would eat.

Blessed be you, perilous matter, violent sea, untamable passion, you who, unless we fetter you, will devour us.

Blessed be you, mighty matter, irresistible march of evolution, reality ever new-born, you who, by constantly shattering our mental categories, force us to go even further and further in our pursuit of the truth.

Blessed be you, universal matter, immeasurable time, boundless ether, triple abyss of stars and atoms and generations, you who by overflowing and dissolving our narrow standards or measurements reveal to us the dimensions of God.

Blessed be you, impenetrable matter, you who interposed between our minds and the world of essences, cause us to languish with the desire to pierce through the seamless veil of phenomena.

Blessed be you, mortal matter, you who one day will undergo the process of dissolution within us and will thereby take us forcibly into the very heart of that which exists.

You who batter us and then dress our wounds, you who resist and yield to us, you who wreck and build, you who shackle and liberate, the sap of our souls; the hand of God, the flesh of Christ, it is you, matter, that I bless.

3. Stressed Out?

Dr. Fred Alan Wolf gives me insight and remembrance with his words below. By changing my thoughts about who I am, I can begin to integrate my spirit and physical matter into a free flowing unit of being. Stress becomes the contrast that I accept and forgive and move through, on my way to total self-awareness and higher vibrations. It seems my quest in physical form is to reconnect my body with my body-less spirit, in order to reduce the illusion of suffering. A reunion of selves reduces my need for external props and the drama I experience is more joy than suffering.

"Much like Narcissus who was punished by the Goddess Nemesis for resisting Echo's call, spirit embedded in matter as self-meaning body consciousness-resists spirit's call. In doing so, embodied spirit makes a primary distinction: recognizing itself as matter, it becomes entranced, lost in the image of itself as separate from spirit; an illusion, and a powerful one. Thus we, as self, begin the lifelong process of distinguishing one thing from another, a process from which we derive both joy and suffering.

Narcissus dies at the edge of the river gazing at his own reflection. Each of us suffers a similar malady as we gaze intently at the image we call our bodies. Unlike Narcissus, however, we don't just lie there, lost in our reflection. We move on, all the while feeling the loss as we miss the echo of our spirit calling us. We live in continual stress arising from the anxiety of the ongoing battle between matter and spirit (body and soul). Some of you may object to this idea, claiming through special techniques, meditation, spiritual practice, or simply being a good person, we may experience relief from this stress. But like the suffering of Narcissus, the stress I refer to must continually arise from spirit and body opposing each other. The battle results in a continual conflict we all feel as our common human suffering.

Ironically, it is this very condition that makes life worthwhile and leads to the wonderful drama of our daily reality.

Our human condition depends on the rise of spiritual stress. And here the mind enters the game. More than any other causative factor, our thoughts amplify this stress. More important than any medical care, good mental habits promote relief from this stress amplification. By good mental habits I mean simply thinking positively about every situation we encounter, even when critical thought is required."

4. A Thousand Years Forgotten

Sometimes when a bird cries out,
Or the wind sweeps through a tree,
Or a dog howls in a far off farm.
I hold still and listen a long time.

My world turns and goes back to the place
Where a thousand forgotten years ago,
The bird and the blowing wind
Were like me, and were my brothers.

My soul turns into a tree,
And an animal, and a cloud bank.
Then changed and odd it comes home
And asks me questions. What should I reply?

Hermann Hesse was born in 1877. He was a German author, poet, novelist, and painter. In 1946, he received the Nobel Peace Prize in Literature. Best known for his works *Steppenwolf, Siddhartha,* and *The Glass Bead Game,* Hesse made an individual search for spirituality outside of society. His work became popular in the U.S. counterculture revolution of the 1960s known as the Hippie Movement.

Hesse's poem asks an important question: How should I reply to my soul? Do I continue to see and feel the world around me as a separate entity, or will I accept the fact that I am connected to all life? Do I continue to treat the earth as a ball of water and air sitting in a universe of mystery, or do I become aware of the greater blueprint of life? All my past years have brought me to this point of now. Now is the moment of discovery where I merge my soul with ALL THERE IS in the magnificent unity of being.

Today is a cause for celebration. It's a day of awakening. I am changing into a grander version of myself and my family of consciousness is nudging me to accept it. Each New Year brings enlightenment and little by little I feel my life expand from three dimensions into four or five, and even more when I'm ready. Moving through time and space seems faster now; I sense the magic of my Creator in all my actions. I rejoice in every moment and thank the eternal Goddess for the ability to change and become a grander physical image of her.

My answer is another question. It will always be another question. In the question I find another aspect of myself. I feel the power that rests within me and I am grateful for it. Living in the now brings me closer to the essence of being one with the bird, the tree, the cloud, and my own consciousness.

5. A Word about Nothing

We shape clay into a pot, but it is the emptiness inside that holds whatever we want.

That idea was expressed by Lao Tzu over 2,500 years ago in his writing known as the *Tao Te Ching.*

Emptiness or "nothingness" has been written about for centuries, and explained in many ways. It has been the foundation of many beliefs and cultures and continues to draw us into its presence. When I read anything that pertains to spirituality, "nothing" is the topic that is discussed most. Nothing is everything, yet I do not perceive it with my physical senses, nor can I grasp it with my physical form. This something, which is nothing, is all consuming and pervasive and it is an art form within itself.

Artur Schnabel, the great 20th century pianist explained his gift this way, *"The notes I handle no better than many pianists. But, the pauses between the notes—ah, that is where the art resides."*

Leonardo Da Vinci said, *"Among the great things, which are to be found among us, the being of Nothingness is the greatest."*

In Zen teachings, *"Even a good thing isn't as good as nothing."* John Cage, the American composer said, *"I have nothing to say, I am saying it, and that is poetry."*

Nothingness is the art behind the art, and it expresses itself through everything.

So, this great nothing is an artist that resides within me and expresses itself through my creations and the creations of all life. It is the master artist that is nothing but a massive particle of everything. How awesome! The definition of nothing is awe inspiring for it contains the essence of existence. It is the power to create, change and expand into a grander version of the awe of everything.

But, my definition of nothing is not complete, for nothing is changing even as I write this. It is expanding into something else through my thoughts and the thoughts of those who read this. I can only feel it and be at peace with myself knowing there is more than meets the eye of physical form.

The French poet Paul Valery explains it this way: *"God made everything out of nothing, but the nothingness shows through."*

6. Being is What?

*A painting by Van Gogh. A pair of rough peasant shoes,
nothing else. Actually, the painting represents nothing. But, as
to what is in that picture, you are immediately alone with it as
though you yourself were making your way wearily homeward
with your hoe on an evening in late fall after the last potato fires
have died down. What is here? The canvas? The brush strokes?
The spots of color?*

Martin Heidegger was born in 1889 in Germany. He is considered
one of the great philosophers of the 20th century. Many of the
minds before him wrote about being, but never really defined it.
His work, *Being and Time*, sought to answer that question.
He tried to define being in human terms and his work influenced
many thinkers, including Jean-Paul Sartre.

I look at his quote above and realize that the world is much like
the Van Gogh painting. I see and feel what I perceive it to be.
I can see a blank canvas, with nothing there for me to experience.
I can see an old pair of shoes and believe they are someone else's
shoes, not mine. Or, I can see the shoes and the canvas and make
up my own story about them, just as Heidegger did. All of this is
up to me, through my thoughts and my being.

The interesting thing is my world consists of so many paintings
like this one, many probabilities for me to choose from.
What shall I be today; the shoes or the canvas or the brush?

Co-creation is not a new term. I do it daily in my work and
leisure activities. I rarely think about me co-creating my
world and everything in it. I have been trained to think about
separation. Something or someone is manifesting this world
and I am just living in the process. I have no say in how my
life evolves, God or fate or chance or genes have control of

my journey. They paint the canvas of my life, not me. I see
the results and wonder why it looks a certain way, and blame
someone or something else if I don't like the end result.

Creation is a term used in defining God, the creator of all things.
I am part of his creation, but show few signs of my creator. I can
see why Heidegger was so hell-bent on defining being. What is
the point of being if I have no control over the process?

"Being is" has been a phrase used to describe the art of living.
"Being without being," is another way of describing the experience.
There are many more ways to label it, but to me, being is connection.
It is awareness. It understands me not just in human terms but in
spiritual terms as well.

There is so much more to being than I am aware of. I have
many aspects of consciousness that exist outside of this focused
consciousness I call being. I cannot define them all for I have
forgotten them. I am beginning now to remember, to expand
and grow. In order to remember I have freedom, free will and
the ability to think. Thoughts create matter. They create my world.
If I believe that, I am a co-creator of my being. I am able to
use my canvas and create a being aligned with what I believe. If I
remember I am a spirit having a human experience, I am able to
redefine and change my being.

Being human is one brush stroke of my consciousness, not the
complete work of art. Each thought adds another stroke to
the canvas. The canvas is unending, the paint is ever flowing
and the work is never finished. Perfection is changing, as I change.

As Heidegger said in his book, being is always intended towards
something or about something. My being is intended towards
knowing myself in more than human terms. My being is heading
towards remembering who I am, and I get to pick what colors to
use on my canvas.

7. I am Living Art

I found these words written in "The Notebooks of Malte Laurids Brigge," by the twentieth century poet Rainer Maria Rilke:

For poems are not, as people think, simply emotions- they are experiences.

For the sake of a single poem, you must see many cities, many people and things,

You must understand animals, must feel how birds fly,

And know the gestures, which small flowers make when they open in the morning.

You must be able to think back to streets in unknown neighborhoods,

To unexpected encounters, and to partings you had long seen coming;

to days of childhood whose mystery is still unexplained,

to parents whom you had to hurt when they brought in a joy and you didn't pick it up;

To childhood illnesses that began so strangely

With so many profound and difficult transformations,

To days in quiet, restrained rooms and to mornings by the sea,

To the sea itself, to seas,

*To nights of travel that rush along high overhead and went flying
with all the stars,*

*And it is still not enough to be able to think of all that.
You must have memories of many nights of love,*

Each one different from all the others,

Memories of women screaming in labor,

*And of light, pale, sleeping girls who have just given birth and
are closing again.*

But you must also have been beside the dying,

*Must have sat beside the dead in the room with the open window
and scattered noises.*

And it is not yet enough to have memories.

You must be able to forget them when they are many,

And you must have the immense patience to wait until they return.

For the memories themselves are not important.

Only when they have changed into our very blood,

Into glance and gesture, and are nameless,

No longer to be distinguished from ourselves-

Only then can it happen

That in some very rare hour

*The first word of a poem arises in their midst
And goes forth from them.*

There is poetry in all of us. My existence in physical form is living art. Rilke points out that my daily experiences are the ingredients that create poetic expression. I overlook many of them; cast them off as nothingness, but everything has purpose. My life is a living poem, a collection of open verse for me to enjoy and cherish. I make it real. I make it true by my thoughts and beliefs. To know the meaning of poetry, I only need to look within myself to feel the power that my energy source gives me. I only need to express my innate love of all life and be thankful for that opportunity. I only need to realize that I am just one word in the poem of infinity that endlessly continues to write grand verses. I only need to remember who I am to become the expression of my creator. Rilke's words help me understand that every moment I create a beautiful poem. Now is the time to become my poetry.

8. *Birds Don't Resemble Eggs*

Jalaluddin Rumi was born in Afghanistan in 1207. His family consisted of scholars, jurists and theologians. He and his family fled Afghanistan to avoid the Mongol invasions and settled in Konya, Turkey. He was the original whirling dervish, a dance of surrender that is still practiced in some religious ceremonies around the world.

Several western scholars have translated Rumi's message of love and unity. I found this piece in Coleman Barks book Rumi We Are Three. The book is dedicated to people in the San Francisco area, who attended one of Barks' readings in 1986. The messages in the book are for everyone from every faith and every belief.

Representatives from Christian, Jewish, Muslim and other religions attended Rumi's funeral in 1273 to honor the works and life of this great teacher. His message united the spirits of all faiths and he is still uniting people from all corners of the world with his love and truth.

I am grateful for finding Rumi. He has changed my thoughts and has helped me remember who I Am—a spirit having a human experience.

From Rumi's Mathnawi III: 3494-3516, enjoy this food for thought:

A friend remarks to the Prophet, "Why is it I get screwed in business deals? It's like a spell. I become distracted by business talk and make wrong decisions."

The Prophet replies, "Stipulate with every transaction that you need three days to make sure."

*Deliberation is one of the qualities of God. Throw a dog a bit of
something. He sniffs to see if he wants it. Be that careful.
Sniff with your wisdom nose. Get clear. Then decide.*

*The universe came into being gradually. God could have just
commanded, "Be!" Little by little a person reaches forty and
fifty and sixty, and feels more complete. God could have thrown
full blown prophets flying through the cosmos in an instant.
Jesus said one word, and a dead man sat up, but creation
usually unfolds, like calm breakers. Constant, slow movement
teaches us to keep working like a small creek that stays clear,
that doesn't stagnate, but finds a way through numerous details,
deliberately. Deliberation is born of joy, like a bird from an egg.*

*Birds don't resemble eggs! Think how different the hatching
is—a white leathery snake egg, a sparrow's egg, a quince seed,
an apple seed—very different things look similar in early stages.*

*These leaves, our bodily personalities, seem identical, but the
globe of soul fruit we make, each is elaborately unique.*

9. I Found it by Myself

Somebody showed it to me and I found it by myself.

Lew Welch the American Beat Generation poet was born in 1926. He taught a poetry workshop at the University Of California Extension in San Francisco from 1965 to 1970. His work started what became known as the "San Francisco Renaissance."

Lew's words fill a mind with thoughts. In order to be awakened, someone or something needs to be the awaker and that usually is a jolting experience. Certainly waking from a deep sleep by an alarm does take a bit of getting used to, but gradually I adjust my thoughts to expect the wake up call. Years of education explain the ways of life and how it has been lived and what to expect in my lifetime. History has a way of repeating itself, or so the story goes; everything repeats itself in the manner of new thoughts; I, based on what has been shown me by others, create a cycle of life.

What if there is another life waiting for me to show it something; another reality where I am the only one in the presence of a multitude of probabilities. This reality is filled with dreams and a blueprint of all life that is connected to a cosmos of consciousness. What if that is where I develop the thoughts for the reality I express in physical form? My words and actions reflect my free will and I do show this reality how I create myself. I can choose from the dreams and probabilities from my other reality and become a thinking form in this time/space world. Now that's an interesting thought and one that I was never taught, but then how do I even think such a thing if no one showed it to me; unless I found it by myself.

The Zen Master Sokei-an Sasaki explains the question this way:

One day I wiped out all notions from my mind. I gave up all desires. I discarded all the words with which I thought and stayed in quietude. I felt a little queer- as if I were being carried into something, or as if I were touching some power unknown to me... and Ztt! I entered. I lost the boundary of my physical body. I had my skin, of course, but I felt I was standing in the center of the cosmos. I spoke, but my words had lost their meaning. I saw people coming toward me, but all were the same man. All were myself! I had never known this world. I had believed that I was created, but now I must change my opinion: I was never created; I was the cosmos; no individual existed.

So, here I am filled with thoughts of another reality and living in this one as well. How many more realities will I discover connected in this web of consciousness? How many more lives will I live by going within myself and exploring my cosmos? The answers wait for me, for I am the question that is filled with answers.

10. The Truth Is...

*"The truth is that life is hard and dangerous; that those who seek
their own happiness do not find it; that those who are weak must
suffer; that those who demand love will be disappointed; that
those who are greedy will not be fed; that those who seek peace
will find strife; that truth is only for the brave; that joy is only
for those who do not fear to be alone; that life is only for the one
who is not afraid to die."*

Joyce Cary, the Irish novelist and artist was born in 1888.
Cary's words describe the attitude of the 20th century, and most
of the centuries before it, because life was hard and dangerous.
Living in almost complete separation from the reality of spirit, the
weak suffered, and the greedy became greedier. The peacemakers
were warriors that tried to overcome strife by creating wars.
The truth was a lie, joy was a fleeting thought and almost everyone
was afraid to die. This age of separation began to unravel in the
mid 20th century and a new age began to appear.

The new age is really not so new; it is more an awakening than
it is new knowledge. Many centuries before life was recorded,
this age of awareness flourished and people lived in harmony
within themselves. Countless tales have been told of ancient
civilizations that were self reliant, self aware and connected
to their higher self on a daily basis. Truth was what they lived;
happiness was a gift they gave to themselves; weakness was a
temporary state of mind that was corrected by asking for help;
greed was a selfless act which created dis-ease; love was not
demanded, it was a natural state of being; peace had no opposite
and death was the reconnection of consciousness to a grander
state of existence.

These civilizations spent many linear years in joy and freedom.
They had abilities that we call super powers, but they were

commonplace in those times. Mental telepathy, self-healing, astral travel and long physical lives made up the DNA of these distant relatives of mine. The sense of self worth was practiced daily in acts of gratitude, forgiveness and kindness. Children were regarded as angels that brought change and new energy to the planet. Everyone lived to change and appreciate the growth that expansion brings. Laws were etched in the psyche of each entity and everyone agreed before birth to honor them. Work was a privilege that fulfilled the desire of each soul and guaranteed the reincarnation of spirit in other manifestations.

This new age is back once again; it is the age of consciousness, the blending of multi-dimensional realities into one experience. This glorious adventure will take me to a place of remembering where I reunite with the other aspects of myself. I am able to control my emotions and use my impulses to make conscious decisions. I accept contrast as a tool for growth and use my truth with pleasure. The feeling of unity surrounds me and I treat all life as precious and know that everything has consciousness. My energy is filled with love from the source of all energy and I appreciate it with acts of compassion. My spirit brings me to the doorway of abundance and I walk through it with confidence. I am truly free once again to live in the essence of All There Is and thank myself for the opportunity.

The 21st century is my now and it is the beginning of the old way of believing. No longer burdened with useless judgment I can be who I really am, a spirit having a human experience and feel the love that I came from and live in harmony with myself.

11. Good Morning

Mornings are a good time for me to collect my thoughts and to enjoy feeling good about myself. Another day awaits me with a fresh chain of events full of expectation. Choices of every kind wait for me. I can be what I desire, or I can desire not to be. The solitude of morning brings emotions in focus and I can see a world that is mine to enjoy. It is a wonderful time to share love with all life and be grateful for the abundance that surrounds me. This morning, I opened a book of thoughts that I had put together several years ago when I was studying poets from different worlds. Two of my favorite poets were in front of me. Each one reminded me of the different choices I can make. The first is by Mevlana Celaleddin Rumi:

This being human is a guest house; every morning a new arrival. A joy, a depression, meanness, some momentary awareness comes as an unexpected visitor. Welcome and entertain them all, even if they're a crowd of sorrows, who violently sweep your house empty of its furniture. Still treat each guest honorably; he may be cleaning you out for some new delight. The dark thought, the shame, the malice, meets them all at the door laughing and invites them in. Be grateful for whoever comes, because each has been sent, as a guide from beyond.

The second is by Rainer Maria Rilke.

It feels as though I make my way through massive rock like a vein of ore alone, encased. I am so deep inside it I can't see the path or any distance. Everything is close and everything closing in on me has turned to stone. Since I still don't know enough about pain, this terrible darkness makes me small. If it's you though; press down hard on me, break in, that I may know the weight of your hand, and you the fullness of my cry.

"Vielleicht Dab Ich Durch Schwere Berge Gehe"

12. Here's to a New Level of Thinking

We can't solve a problem at the same level of thinking that created it.

Albert Einstein opened a new level of thinking to science and the world. His life had focus and purpose as he worked diligently to solve problems at a different level of thinking. Thanks to his work, a new window of knowing was opened and thoughts came flowing in at the speed of light. I can only imagine what Einstein's world was like, but I can know exactly what my world contains.

In the scientific community, new thoughts are emerging to solve some of the mysteries it faces. Quantum physics, which was introduced towards the end of Einstein's life, has changed a lot of the facts we once accepted as true, and has answered some questions that fascinated Einstein.

Various religious groups are being asked to answer some old questions that have surfaced about the foundations of their beliefs. New evidence is shining light on many of the facts we took as gospel. The church may not have been as candid as some of us would like; for others, it makes no difference. A belief is a belief, right?

Yes, a belief is a belief and we all have different thoughts that become our beliefs. Through them, we live our lives, and experience and express ourselves in so many ways. That is our choice and should be respected. We are not here to solve all of the problems we encounter, but to learn and grow from them. I can make a difference, if I change my thinking to another level. It is my task to work on my beliefs and myself. I can't change anyone else without his or her consent, but I have everything I need to be the change I want to see in my own life.

Like Einstein, I can find new discoveries within myself to elevate my thinking. I realize that there is more to me than what I see in this dimension. Contrary to what modern medicine believes, my mind, body and spirit are not separate from me. I am connected to all life and everything has an effect upon me. The God I call creator is my mind, body and spirit, but it is so much more. This awareness brings me to a higher place of consciousness. From that place, I can begin to solve the problems I created with limiting beliefs.

Feeling one with ALL THERE IS, gives me the power to attract whatever I need into my life. Everything is there waiting for me to simply allow it. There are no problems big enough to disconnect me from my Source or destroy me. I can move myself through the twenty-first century in joy. I am grateful for understanding and accepting each problem. By reaching for a better thought, problems become the tools of growth.

Einstein lived in his world. I live in mine. Each of us has the ability to be the solution instead of a problem. As the physicist Amit Goswami said, "When we understand us, our consciousness, we also understand the universe and the separation disappears."

Here's to a new level of thought!

13. Twilight

*Twilight is a time for sharing; and a time for remembering;
remembering the things of beauty wasted by our careless hands;
our frequent disregard of other living things; the many songs
unheard because we would not listen.*

*Listen tonight with all the wisdom of your spirit; listen too with
all the compassion of your heart; lest there come another night;
when there is only silence. A great and total silence.*

Winston Abbott's words are true. Twilight is the time for sharing
and remembering. There are many twilights to experience in
physical life. The daily setting of the sun over the horizon brings
the day to an end and night begins. This certainly is a time to
reflect on my day's activities and remember who I am. There is
the twilight of my career and all the work I have done to find a
place in this world of materialism. This is the time to share what
I have learned from that journey. Then, there is the twilight of
my life where I remember family and friends, ambitions and
accomplishments, fears and conquests, and loves of times past.
I reflect on my life and am able to feel the joy and laughter,
agony and pain, lust and fulfillment that my thoughts created for me.
I begin to listen to voices that have always been present, but I
had refused to hear. I begin to listen to the wisdom of my spirit.

Hindsight they say is 20-20. I have the ability to see myself
after the fact much better than when I am in the present moment.
I am able to correct my mistakes and forgive myself for the
acts of selfishness, greed and fruitless words that pop out of fear.
I am able to remember why I acted in a manner that was not
compassionate and why I separated myself from the living
things around me. I am able to see the waste and neglect that I
participated in so that I could be accepted as a human. I am able
to change my thoughts and begin to live the way my spirit lived

before I put it in another dimension. I am able to be me at any time of twilight, if I believe I can.

Abbott says listen to the silence; the great and total silence of being in sync with my spirit. Within the silence is a great resting place that holds all the beauty and gracefulness of twilight. I begin to hear the songs that have always been sung; I begin to see what I know is true; I feel my emotions and follow my heart with quiet fortitude. I experience the total aspect of human form and express myself in gratitude. I become the "me" I came to earth to be, and rejoice in knowing who I really am. I am one with the twilight—one with the universe in a web of love that expands and grows as I remember.

Twilight is a time for sharing and remembering. Twilight is now; it happens in the inner world of spirit. There is no need to wait for linear time to awaken me. I am in the web of connection and always will be, I just need to use it. My thoughts are filled with the web of remembering—the magic remedy for what ails me. Tapping into the silence that flows freely through me, is the gift of life. I can open it at anytime. The sun and the horizon are infinitely one within me. Twilight is the physical and spiritual art of unity, unity with all life in peace.

™

The Self

1. A Heart Full Of Honey

I dreamt last night, oh marvelous error, that there were
honeybees in my heart, making honey out of my old failures.

Antonio Machado was born in Seville, Spain in 1875. He was
a Spanish poet and one of the leading figures in the Spanish
literary movement known as the Generation of '98.

Antonio's idea of turning his failures into productive experiences
is an important one. I have had many failures through the years
and each one has not only taught me something about myself,
it also encouraged me to continue my journey of remembering
with my eyes open and my heart full of honey.

As I look back on these failures, I see them as lessons that I
created for myself. At the time I didn't blame myself for them,
there was always someone or something else to blame; I never
caused the suffering and pain I went through by the choices
I had made. I never had the insight to see what I was doing
to myself. The world was a big, bad place and I was a victim
of circumstances and luck. I failed to feel my truth, and went
blindly into situations that could only have one outcome.

Failure is a word I feared, and that was what I focused my
attention on. I was always in a state of fear, and I attracted that
experience into my physical life. I did not go into these ventures
with love in my heart. I was filled with illusions, and the end
result was filled with what I expected. What I asked for, I was given.

I know now that each act I labeled as failure was a blessing
waiting for me to accept it. They became part of the "me" that
accepts all the choices I have made.

All of my thoughts have gotten me where I am now. Through the pain and suffering I was able to change my thoughts and focus on the honey in my heart. I was able to forgive myself and ask forgiveness from those I may have hurt by my choices. I was able to grow into a grander version of the self that had been hidden in the fear of failure. This grander version of me accepts responsibility for the choices I make and lives them without fear. I am the bee who creates honey in my heart and shares it in gratitude.

Now, I treat success and failure as natural experiences on my journey. I fill every choice with love and I dress myself in truth. My truth is to be the connected spirit traveling a physical journey, to grow from the contrast of being human, and expand from the experience. I do this filled with the freedom and awareness of ALL THERE IS, Love.

2. A Loftier Race?

These things shall be—a loftier race
Than e'er the world hath known shall rise
With flame of freedom in their souls,
And light of knowledge in their eyes.

John Symonds was born in 1914. He was an English novelist,
playwright and author of children's books. His message of a
loftier race sounds like it came from a children's book; a thought
that kids take to heart and imagine to be real. When I was a
kid, I liked to read about such myths and fantasies. I put myself
in such dreams and lived there for a while. It was a pleasant
experience to find myself living in another form if only for a
minute or two. It almost seemed real to me and then I later
discovered it was real.

Ken Wilbur, one of our modern day philosophers, explains
something about self this way:

Notice what it is that you call "you"- you might notice two parts
of this "self": one, there is some sort of observing self, an inner
subject or watcher; and two, there is some sort of observed self,
some objective things that you can see or know about yourself,
such as I am a father, mother, doctor, clerk etc. The first is
experienced as an "I," the second as a "me" or even mine.
The first self is the proximate self since it is closer to "you"; and
the second is the distant self since it is objective and farther away.
Both of them together, along with other sources of selfness are
called the overall self.

Ken's thoughts and Symonds' poem are related in the fact that
my inner self is now watching my distant self become a flame
of knowledge. This knowledge is the awareness of my inner self
that I had buried many years before with the shovel of fear. I was

scared to listen or follow this "I" within me and I allowed the external world to mold me in physical form. So my "I" was tied to the chair of dualism and waited for my "me" to untie the ropes and free my soul.

This freedom is enlightenment. It knows both parts of myself and remembers who I am. It is realizing that this journey through time and space is the playground of dreams; it is the theater for the play I wrote for myself; it is the manifestations of my thoughts and the time to connect to that loftier race John writes about.

We are all part of that enlightened race, the race with freedom in our souls; the race with the knowledge of eternity in our hearts; the race with love overflowing in our bodies and minds; the race that is a whole part of another whole that is connected to ALL THERE IS.

If I believe I am those things, I will experience them physically. I will express them physically and I will become what I believe. Just like the kid who dreamed about grander places and bigger adventures, I become part of the loftier race. That race offers itself in unconditional service to all life and expresses gratitude for the opportunity to be a grander version of the self that is united to all consciousness.

3. Am I a Bird or a Worm?

If you always do what you always did, you'll always get what you always got.

That quote has been said in many different ways over the years. It reminds me that I live in a world of growth and change. In order to grow, I must change. William Blake put it this way: "The man who never alters his opinion is like standing water, and breeds reptiles of the mind."

Yes, Blake did have a way with words and thoughts. I do become stagnant when I close my mind and only believe what I have always believed because my world changes both internal and external by the second.

Walt Whitman said it this way: *"Do I contradict myself?* Very well then... I contradict myself; I am large... I contain multitudes."

Right, there are many aspects of my consciousness. There are many forms of "me" wrapped up in this body. How many do I know and love? I am certainly not the same me I was 30 years ago, and my world is not the same either. My beliefs have changed and I have grown into another me. I have created a me that fits my beliefs. What I see in the mirror is pure creation. I am continually changing in order to be a grander version of myself—to learn how to love and share it with all life. Each event I face gives me that opportunity. How I express myself is my choice, and it becomes who I am. What I think I am is who I am. What do I want to experience? What do I want to express? What do I want to become?

I know who I am, and I am growing in that knowledge of awareness. Shel Silverstein in his book, Where the Sidewalk Ends, wrote "Early Bird," which tells me how to express myself if I become a bird or a worm.

Oh, if you're a bird, be an early bird
And catch the worm for your breakfast plate.
If you're a bird, be an early bird-
But if you're a worm, sleep late.

There are so many things I can be, because all my selves are connected to the Divine Matrix of ALL THERE IS, Love. And, love is all things.

4. A Puddle of Illusions

The mind does not shine by its own light. It too is an object, illumined by the self... But the self is boundless. It is pure consciousness that illuminates the contents of the mind... Egoism, the limiting sense of I results from the individual intellect's attributing the power of consciousness to itself.

Patanjali is the compiler of the Yoga Sutra, a major work containing philosophical aspects of mind and consciousness. The date of the work is around 200 BC. Patanjali is known as the founder of Yoga, although the science of uniting one's consciousness is found in other works of Hindu scriptures that are older than that. Patanjali's work serves as the basis of the yoga-system known as Raja Yoga. What was obscure, Patanjali clarified. What was abstract, he made practical, inspiring a long line of teachers and practitioners.

The essence of Yoga is just now being understood in Western thought. The connection of various selves that makes me a whole self is beginning to be accepted in modern society. The concept of pure consciousness filling my mind and body has been around for thousands of years, and yet I was never taught to think that way.

Religion told me I was a separate being with no connection to my Source other than through religion. Religion told me that it was the vehicle needed to reconnect me to my Source. However, now I know that I was never disconnected from my Source. When I changed my beliefs, my world changed. That is what Patanjali's message explains. I gave my power to the self that existed in physical form—the self that didn't understand why I was experiencing life in this time/space world.

I searched for answers everywhere around me, but because I thought I was separate from nature, other life, and even from my creator, I sat in a puddle of illusions, dripping with fear. This was my birth of egoism.

Enlightenment is the towel that dries my fears. By enlightenment, I mean unity within myself; remembering other aspects of this being I call human. Remembering I am not only an ego, but I am another consciousness, perhaps a group of consciousnesses that is connected to a stream of ALL THERE IS, Love.

I can change how I experience my physical journey. I can create a world of peace and freedom by expressing the other aspects of my consciousness. I free myself from the feelings of separation that my ego created. I become a whole part of another whole, aware that I am expressing my humanity to become a grander version of the spirit that is an eternal child sitting on the threshold of infinity.

5. *A Spotless Mind*

Blessed is he who expects nothing for he shall never be disappointed.

Alexander Pope was born in 1688 in London, and is considered one of the greatest writers of the eighteenth-century. His quotes have been used as messages from another consciousness.

We are all taught to expect something when we perform an act. My life is based on expectations and the fact that I deserve something in return for my efforts. Pope reminds me that this way of thinking is ego-based desire that leads me to the world of disappointment. I could spend years in this self-imposed jail of depression until I unlock my cell with simple acts of kindness.

The question is why should I do, and not expect reward or reaction? After all, I am here to accumulate and control the things I want; it is my duty to be the richest and most powerful being I can be, right? I see it all around me: on the news, in the books I read and in the movies I watch. My survival depends on how many lies I tell myself in order not to be disappointed. I am a creation of my thoughts and I must fight and drive myself to the edge of destruction in order to be recognized by the world.

Pope thought another way. He knew that my greatest accomplishment would be to know who I am. He knew that by offering my unconditional service to others I would free myself. When I act without expectation, I'm never disappointed. The nothing that comes is everything when I see it as it is—an expression of another aspect of myself. This awareness brings a whole new meaning to the word "nothing," for it is filled with the essence of life. Life is love. Life is the experience of being a human that allows me to become a grander version of the spirit I am.

Pope expressed many thoughts that have become universal ideas:

*And all who told it added something new; and all who heard it
made enlargements too.*

*He who tells a lie is not sensible of how great a task he
undertakes; for he must be forced to invent twenty more to
maintain that one.*

*Our passions are like convulsive fits, which, though they make
us stronger for a time, leave us the weaker ever after.*

This one that sums up the meaning of nothing:

*How happy is the blameless vestal's lot!
The world forgetting, by the world forgot.
Eternal sunshine of the spotless mind!
Each pray'r accepted and each wish resign'd.*

6. Green and Blue Make Turquoise

There is no greater illusion than fear, no greater wrong than preparing to defend yourself, no greater misfortune than having an enemy. Whoever can see through all fear will always be safe.

The immortal words of Lao-tzu, who wrote the Tao Te Ching, which means the book of the way, perfectly captures our need for change.

No one is really sure when he was born, but he is said to be older than Confucius, who was born around 551 B.C. We have lost the idea of things being accomplished without fearing them. Global warming is a prime example. The greening of the world is a noble endeavor, something that requires love, not fear, to incorporate.

The red flag is flying around the world, our climate is changing, but what we are not noticing is that we are changing. Our collective thoughts are changing, and the matter we create through our thoughts is shaping our world. At any given moment we can change our thoughts and change what we experience in our world, including how we perceive the effect of global warming on our lives. If I fear it, that is what I will manifest, as well as all the negativity that is attached to it. If I love it, I will manifest love. My choice of how I want to feel about this issue will be my reality. Which thought feels better?

Our history has painted a picture of defending ourselves, fighting ourselves and killing the enemy, which is also our self. In order to embrace something we must first be at war with it because we fear it. We think it's something that is outside our control and we must conquer it to acquire it. As Lao-tzu says, by seeing through the fear we are safe. It is time for history to stop repeating itself.

There are many things we can do on a personal level as well as a collective group to embrace global warming and deal with it, not only on a green level, but on a turquoise level as well. By integrating thoughts of love and prayer, the sense of seeing things the way we want them to exist is a powerful weapon. If we use our consciousness, not just the focus consciousness but our intuitive knowledge, we can manifest a change. We can demonstrate that we are evolving into that grander version of our self. The contrast of global warming is the catalyst for our change in awareness and connection.

As Rumi said, *"You are the secret of God's secret. You are the mirror of divine beauty. Everything in the universe is within you. Ask all from yourself. The one whom you are looking is also you."*

7. The Snake-Catcher and the Frozen Snake

Listen to this and hear the mystery inside:

*A snake-catcher went into the mountains to find a snake. He wanted
a friendly pet, and one that would amaze audiences, but he
was looking for a reptile, something that has no knowledge of
friendship. It was winter.*

*In the deep snow he saw a frighteningly huge dead snake. He was
afraid to touch it, but he did. In fact, he dragged the thing into
Baghdad; hoping people would pay to see it. This is how foolish
we've become! A human being is a mountain range! Snakes are
fascinated by us! Yet we sell ourselves to look at a dead snake.
We are like beautiful satin used to patch burlap. "Come see the
dragon I killed, and hear the adventures!" That's what he
announced, and a large crowd came, but the dragon was not
dead, just dormant! He set up his show at the crossroads.*

*The ring of gawking people got thicker, everybody on tiptoe,
men and women, noble and peasant, all packed together
unconscious of their differences. It was like a resurrection!
He began to unwind the thick ropes and remove the cloth
coverings he'd wrapped it so well in.*

*Some little movement. The holy Iraqi sun had woken the
terrible life. The people nearest started screaming. Panic!
The dragon tore easily and hungrily loose, killing many instantly.
The snake catcher stood there, frozen. "What have I brought out
of the mountains?" The snake braced against a post and crushed
the man and consumed him.*

*The snake is your animal soul. When you bring it into the hot
air of your wanting-energy warmed by that and by the prospect*

of power and wealth, it does massive damage. Leave it in the snow mountains. Don't expect to oppose it with quietness and sweetness and wishing. The nafs don't respond to those, and they can't be killed. It takes a Moses to deal with such a beast, to lead it back, and make it lie down in the snow. But there was no Moses then. Hundreds of thousands died.

That story was written by Rumi over 1,200 years ago. The message within the story is as important today as it was then. With all the destruction taking place around the world, especially in the Middle East, his message is a wakeup call for me now. The sleeping snake has certainly been awakened in that part of the world and it has devoured thousands in its hungry desire for power and wealth. The interesting thing is I knew it would happen; I knew that any act of destruction brings more of the same and repeats itself century after century. Rumi calls it my animal soul; I call it separation from my family of consciousness.

Moses, as Rumi mentions, is the answer to the havoc that separation brings me. I look everywhere for him, but I don't realize that Moses is within me. I can tame the beast of my ego-driven self by asking my Moses for help or asking my family of consciousness for guidance.

The snake is alive in the Middle East, and it's alive around the world. The audience pays to see the snake in action and thousands die in order for me to remember who I am. Moses lives within all mankind and all that is needed for him to help return the snake to the mountain is acceptance and forgiveness. I can share my Moses with everyone in the audience and a connection takes place. One by one the light of awareness shines through and the snake becomes a web of unity. I am asking my Moses for help today and every day, and I believe it is on the way.

When the message is understood, healing will take place. I begin to feel like the mountain that contains and loves all life and rejoices in its unity—a unity of diversity that respects differences and applauds creativity. Change is the food for growth. Love is the fuel of life. I am the energy that expresses peace and embraces expansion in contrast. My snake is content living in the warm water of eternal love.

8. How Am I Marking Time?

We try to evade the question of existence with property, prestige, power, production, fun, and ultimately, by trying to forget that we—that I—exist. No matter how often he thinks of God or goes to church, or how much he believes in religious ideas, if he, the whole man, is deaf to the question of existence, if he does not have an answer to it, he is marking time, and he lives and dies like one of the million things he produces. He thinks of God, instead of experiencing God.

Erich Fromm was born in 1900 in Germany. He was an internationally renowned Jewish-German-American social psychologist, psychoanalyst, and humanistic philosopher. He taught at Michigan State University and New York University and then moved to Switzerland where he continued to write a series of books and maintain his own clinical practice.

Fromm brings several good thoughts to mind concerning my existence in this physical state. Am I here to collect all the things that superficially matter in material form, or am I matter that exists for other reasons? Certainly, existence has been the topic of conversation for centuries, and there are many explanations as to why I am here. I must choose what fits me as far as belief is concerned. That belief will be what I experience.

Two friends of mine were having a discussion the other day about beliefs and how different beliefs have resulted in the deaths of many people. The war waging in the Middle East is a perfect example of this fact. They both agreed on that, but they could not understand that the enemy's beliefs were just as real as theirs. My friends talked about God, but what they knew about their God was completely opposite to what the enemy knew of their God. They had ideas about what God would or wouldn't do. They agreed that one side had to be right in what

God was thinking. The vision of a personalized God separated from man was the basis for their beliefs. It amazed me that they believed that God would conquer the beliefs of others through violence. Both of my friends felt remorse, anger, and fear while having this discussion. They ended by saying, "Those people will learn what the *real* God is like."

As Fromm points out, we spend a lot of time thinking about what God thinks and does, and very little time experiencing God. My existence is not to collect things, but rather to experience them. My existence is not to judge the other man, for there is no other man, if I experience God. The other man is me, and I am here to learn and grow into a grander version of who I am.

I look around me and nature lives in the God experience. It grows and expands by the expression of its creator. It is not separated from its Source; it is the Source expressing itself in splendor. It does not think about itself; it lives in harmony with diversity. The Source of individual life exists in that life and expands from it. In the smallest cell, the existence of its Source is on display and lives through the cell. Why should I be any different? I am a collection of those cells and unless I choose to stop the process, they are constantly changing and growing.

I have free will. I can believe what I feel "me" to be. In that expression, I become an extension of my Source and experience the essence of my existence. My existence is no longer one of separation, but one of unity and awareness. Connected to ALL THERE IS in a matrix of love, I express myself through the abundance of my Source, and share myself in its existence.

9. I've Got To Stop Killing Myself!

Everything must be based on a simple idea. Once we have finally discovered it, (it) will be so compelling, so beautiful, that we will say to one another, yes, how could it have been any different.

These are the words of John Wheeler, a modern day physicist. So what's the idea? I like simple things, especially simple ideas.

John, like many scientists of our twenty-first century, has discovered that we are all connected. In fact, everything is connected, and everything has a consciousness. Yep, right down to the cells in my body. So do rocks, plants, planets and even events. Our collective consciousness—our collective thoughts—has a direct effect on everyone's daily life, including the situations we experience, right down to the weather. I am seeing and reacting to my thoughts. My thoughts create my reality. So, if I think good is more powerful than evil, that is what I will express. If I think the opposite, then that's what I'm projecting to the world.

I come from a universe, God, Source, or whatever name you use. I was taught that this energy source is all good. That energy is within me, and I have the power to use it. My thoughts make that a reality.

I want peace; we all want peace. It is our natural state of being. In order to create peace, I need to remember what peace is. Political or religious history does not teach me to be at peace with myself. It teaches me to fight or be at war in order to find peace. My ancestors killed themselves looking for something that is so easy to find. I am killing myself looking for the same simple thing.

I believe we are all connected, but diverse. We all feel the same emotions. War does not kill consciousness, but it does block my belief that good is more powerful that evil. I linger in a false illusion of good vs. bad, when there is only good. Fear makes me believe evil is more powerful than what I really am. So, I kill myself and the illusion in a cycle that repeats itself.

In order to free myself, I must look at things with a different consciousness, and see myself as I see others—connected to the same good that permeates the universe. If I accept diversity and agree to learn and evolve from it, I am expanding my consciousness and becoming a grander version of myself. My expansion expands the collective good that is the ALL THAT IS.

10. *I am a Protoplasmal Primordial Atomic Globule!*

*I can trace my ancestry back to a protoplasmal primordial
atomic globule. Consequently, my family pride is something
inconceivable. I can't help it. I was born sneering.*

That's from The Mikado a Gilbert and Sullivan comic opera
that opened at the Savoy, in London, in 1885 and ran for 672
performances. It gave Gilbert the opportunity to satirize British
politics and institutions by disguising them as Japanese.
Nothing funnier than holding a mirror up to myself and thinking
I see someone else.

I certainly have a gift for showing my flaws by projecting them
on to someone or something else. Flaws are a sign of weakness
and I have been taught early on not to be weak. It's okay for the
other guy, because he's different in race, color or creed. I must
be the same in order to be powerful. I can't show my true self,
for that doesn't measure up in a judgmental society, so I lie.
I hide in order to fit in. I become what others think I am. So, I
spend a lifetime trying to figure out where I come from.
Where are my power roots? What is my ancestry? Is my family
pride something inconceivable?

Well the good news is, I could trace myself back in time and
become what I believe, if I give myself the chance. I could
change my perceptions of how I want to interact with my world.
I could look at myself as consciousness that is expressing life
in a specific way. I could view everything as love, instead of
segmenting it because my beliefs are distorted. I could look at
myself with both male and female qualities and unite myself
in physical form. I could begin to laugh at myself and forgive
myself for ignorance. I could do all those things if my thoughts
change from lack to abundance, from bad to good, from flawed

to perfect. I will become what I think. I will be the ancestor I'm looking for. I will be the family pride I desire, and find the root of truth wherever I exist.

I am protoplasmal primordial atomic globule, filled with the energy of the universe, here to become a grander version of myself. Realizing who I am expands my vision of my ancestry to include all life, and ALL THERE IS, Love.

11. Mirror, Mirror, Is That Me That I See?

Behold, I send you like sheep among wolves; be ye therefore wise as serpents and gentle as doves.

That's the Gospel of Matthew (10:16), giving me a message that I am just beginning to understand.

It might be easier if everyone was a sheep, or a wolf, or a dove, or a snake. Then, we would all be alike. If that were the case, everyone would be just like me. It would be like looking in the mirror all the time. All I see is the same, all I feel is the same, and all I do is the same. Day after day I stay the same—no change, no diversity, no growth. The mirror never tarnishes, never cracks, and never breaks. Life is a never-ending sameness of consciousness.

Well, thankfully I am different, and all life is different. In collective diversity I seek to experience myself. The first place I look is outside of myself. Education seems to make me believe that all this diversity is not part of me. Even my religious education taught me that I was separated from the God who created me. If I was disconnected from my creator, surely I wasn't connected to anyone or anything else. No sense in that. I lived for many years trying to figure all that out. Then, I woke up.

My life has purpose and meaning when I rediscover or remember who I am. I must look within myself first. My feeling of wholeness has been covered by years of misunderstanding. Knowing that I was never separated brings new meaning to all I experience in the world. If I am connected to God, everyone is connected and everything is happening so I can experience myself and grow from it.

Every person I see as a sheep teaches me that love comes in gentle ways. The wolves I encounter are showing me the wolf that sits within me, the anger, fear, and judgment I carry, but hide. The serpents killing one another as they fight for survival are really me. I am learning another lesson, about killing and death. Doves that fly in pairs and live in unity and trust are showing me that love is ALL THERE IS.

Wherever I focus my attention, I am looking into a mirror — experiencing, expressing, and growing from what I feel. From the diversity, I can achieve that quest. In remembering, I will give and share myself in order to expand. As I expand, my creator expands and the cycle of life repeats itself in love.

12. Look at Me. I'm the Bee, Butterfly, Brook, and Breeze

The bee is not afraid of me, I know the butterfly; the pretty people in the woods receive me cordially. The brook laughs louder when I come, the breezes madder play. Wherefore, mine eyes, thy silver mists? Wherefore, O summer days?

Beautifully written thoughts by Miss Emily Dickinson. She is an inspiration.

Her words touch a world I sometimes forget—a world that looks to be outside of me, but is really connected to the consciousness that I am. Just by stopping and looking around me, I can see a part of me so vividly. It's not what society tells me to look at or to feel, but there it is, waiting for me to love it.

Nature, and all the consciousness that is within it, is connected. I am part of nature, and each bee, butterfly, brook, and breeze is an extension of who I am. It takes only my thoughts to put me in sync with life. The feeling of unity and new birth of spring engulfs me. The vibrant fullness of summer wraps me in the grandeur of well-being. All the trees, plants, insects, and animals come together to express themselves and to expand in the presence of themselves. Each life form is a part of ALL THERE IS, Love incarnating to feel itself in joy. How beautiful! A world created by love.

I can choose not to see that world. I can be caught in the throes of daily turmoil and pain. I can see everything as separate from me—a constant fight for survival. The mighty always win the wars, but who am I fighting besides myself? I can feel unattached, alone, fearful, and angry. I can make each day an uneventful misery. I can feel sick, tired, and restricted. I can let someone else live life for me through distorted truths.

I know which world feels better. I have made my choice and I know who I am. I am spring, summer, fall, and winter. I am filled with the energy of the universe. I'm connected to my source and am a part of ALL THERE IS. I throw myself into the basket of love and share myself in unconditional universal service. I am gratitude and giving, here to express myself in freedom, awareness, connection, and contrast.

I am what you are. Love.

Movement

1. An Ocean Sits Within Me

If you wish to drown, do not torture yourself with shallow water.

This Bulgarian proverb paints a very good picture of life.
Torturing myself seems to be something that comes easy.
Everyday my thoughts take me on a journey that is filled with
the tools of torture. Anger, fear, judgment, to name a few, eat
away at my well-being, and I quietly torture myself with my
daily existence.

I see the folly in the acts of others, and question the stability
of nature. I act selfishly in business and create frivolous work
to hide my laziness. I look at the weak and homeless as low life,
and put them in a box of rejects within my world. I condone acts
of violence, if they suit my need for power, and reject diversity
for the pursuit of pleasure. I drown myself in the shallow water
of egotistical thoughts to satisfy the lack I feel within me.
Slowly I sink in a puddle of untruths and make myself physically
sick and blame it on someone or something else.

I die a slow death in that puddle, but life goes on around me.
My thoughts create and fill that puddle, yet I have the ability to
step out of it and stand on fertile ground. After all, it is just a
puddle not a lake.

An ocean sits within me, filled with exotic creatures of awareness.
It is connected to the floor of infinity that has mountains of
grandeur and fertile valleys of abundance. The colors of truth
swim in this clear water of knowing, and I have access to all the
wisdom these colors hold. Simply by asking for help from my
ocean, a change takes place. I begin to feel the presence of a self
that was hidden by the tools of torture. I strip and jump into the
water of oneness and baptize myself in its splendor. I accept
and forgive myself for my blindness and open new eyes filled

with gratitude. The torture is over and my ocean once again fills my puddle. I die and am reborn in the flowing stream of self-love, where all I see is what I am.

Torture now becomes the meaning of love, and I experience life in an ocean filled with it. I drown in its abundance and share myself in unconditional universal service.

2. Judge Me Not!

One of the easiest things to accomplish is judgment. We are surrounded by it. It starts early in our lives, and continues through our education, business, political and religious activities. It is the one thing we can identify with because it is what causes the most pain.

Judgment segregates our thoughts, our deeds, and our lives into small compartments of existence. I fall victim to focusing on what others are doing and measure it instead of focusing on my own life. I judge myself by the actions of others. I create a world of pain for myself in order to conform in a diverse universe. I can list all the reasons for this thinking, right and wrong, good and bad; we all could, but that is not the point, for then I continue to judge, not discern.

Discernment is simply done by admitting there are many beliefs to choose from and I can choose my belief. When this is achieved there is no room for judgment, no need for judgment. I accept the fact that there are many paths, but I choose the one that is my truth, without the need to compare myself to anyone, or anything. That is enlightenment. Even understanding the new age way of thought, I still see judgment. I hear, "If you don't believe my way, then you are lost or asleep."

We all have our own path and we all experience what we set out to do, which is to learn and grow. There are many roads to enlightenment; it is our choice and our belief and our truth. So my belief is in unity, the unity of discernment. We can all be who we are and co-exist in harmony with all life. I don't need to be labeled in order to be enlightened. I need to be who I am, a spirit having a human experience and enjoy the journey and use as much laughter as I can along the way. Laughter opens my energy centers and allows me the freedom to express who I am. It releases pain and the judgment associated with it.

I was reading a D.T.Suzuki's book this morning and found this quote from Huang-po, who is considered one of the Masters of Zen thought. I use it because he tells us what enlightenment is, of course he uses Buddha as the reference, and that's OK, I can be discerning and put whatever symbol I want to use in Buddha's place. It is the message that resonates, not the religion.

Both the Buddhas and all sentient beings are of one Mind only, and there are no other objects. This mind has no beginning, was never born, and will never pass away; it is neither blue nor yellow; it has no shape, no form; it does not belong to the category of being and non-being; it is not to be reckoned as new or old; it is neither short nor long, neither large or small; it transcends all measurements, name ability, marks of identification, and forms of antithesis. It is absolute thisness; the wavering of a thought at once misses it. It is like a vacuity of space, it has no boundaries, it is altogether beyond calculation.

Huang-Po's words explain why there is no judgment, only enlightenment. I am connected to all life in the web of Love. Love does not judge for it has only one thought.

3. As I Learn, I Change

As we learn we always change, and so our perception. This changed perception then becomes a new Teacher inside each of us.

Hyemeyohsts Storm wrote the book, *Seven Arrows*, in 1972. He grew up in Montana on an Indian reservation and was schooled and guided by his native teachers. Mother Earth is the focal point of his life and all life has purpose and meaning along with the change that is experienced in the process of rebirth.

Change is the only constant I encounter on my physical journey and I usually react to it by being afraid. Fear controls my perceptions and I fight a war within myself in order to function on a daily basis. I know fear because I create it, but I want to disown it and blame something or someone else for my discomfort. I try to avoid it, but it takes on a life of its own and controls my thoughts. So, change becomes frightening and the unknown is a hole of misery where everything I perceive fills it with horror.

I have been taught to fight, to resist the pain that I experience in fear. I do anything I can to do battle with the enemy that sits in my thoughts. I do everything I can to kill it. My teachers show me how to defeat this curse; I fill my closet with medication and bottles of alcohol. My body weakens and my mind becomes distorted from these battles and I long for the relief of death, yet I never express that wish for fear of being called crazy.

Storm was taught to deal with pain in another way. Certainly there were men and women on the reservation who learned how to cope like I did, but Storm's approach was different. When fear gets in the way of healthy changes, Storm talks to the fear, inviting it along with him on his course of action. Getting to know the fear allows him to ask it for a gift: the courage to walk

with fear at his side and learn from it as he goes. It allows him
to learn which fear is blocking his progress and which fear is
healthily cautioning him against actions that might be harmful.
There is no war raging within him. There is only acceptance
and integration.

Storm demonstrates change as a free flowing reality filled with
growth. It is my thoughts that make my journey a winding road
with bumps, or a path filled with land mines. I have a choice;
and from my choices, my perceptions create probabilities.
Those probabilities may be fearful, but I can welcome the fear
as a teacher. I can accept and forgive myself and deal with the
fear by working with it; working through it and understanding
why I created it in the first place. By releasing and allowing it to
manifest, I change immediately and feel my spirit guiding me in
thoughts of peace. I become the change and sense the purpose
of my life, which is to know who I am and to be what I have
always been.

I have many teachers inside me. I have untold changes to experience.
I have more fears to change into love. From the contrast comes
the expansion and I become a grander version of a spirit
having a human experience. I am connected to life in the web
of ALL THERE IS where fear is spelled L O V E.

4. Are You Ready to Make a Leap?

We are on the verge of the new age, a whole new world.
Human consciousness, our mutual awareness, is going to make
a quantum leap. Everything will change... All this is going to
happen just as soon as you're ready.

That quote came from the book *Das Energi*, written by Paul
Williams in 1973. The book was one of those underground
hits that came into its own around 1978. Paul has led a very
interesting life and has been involved in several different
writing projects. He certainly has made his leap, and is
experiencing his self-made world with the zest of quantum energy.

There is a lot of talk about new age or now age spirituality and
what that means to all of us. I know many people misunderstand
what this age is, and there are others who are scared of it.
Change of any kind is hard for most of us; sameness seems so
safe in a world full of monsters.

Our political and religious systems have stayed the same for
centuries, and all I need to do is look around and see what
they have created. For some, it is a heaven; others burn in
the hell of these systems. Both are illusions of one reality.
Everyone has a choice about how to feel good, and we have been
conditioned to feel safe in numbers. Numbers don't lie right?
I guess it depends on what numbers we're talking about, but I
would say even our number system is questionable.

If I weigh the good and bad, right and wrong of my typical way
of life, it all leads me back to myself. I bought into numbers,
politics, religion and a world of other beliefs because someone
told me that was the way I should think. Not thinking like the

rest of the pack, made me an outcast from group thinking and in some cases, I could be called disturbed. I think disturbed fits as one description for me.

Disturbed because I lost my truth somewhere in the group. I was something someone else created, dressed in conformity. I was covered in fear and was gasping for change. There was no one to relieve me from my pain, but myself, and I have done that.

Back in the 70's Paul Williams felt the need to find himself. He went inside his thoughts and overhauled them, so he could catch the wave of the new age. He believed that by changing what he thought, he could make a difference in his world. He was not concerned with anyone else and how they thought, that was their choice and he respected it. He made the quantum leap at his pace, it just happened to be in his time of the now age.

We all will become of age when we choose to look within ourselves and discover there is more to our consciousness than physical achievement. There is more to reality than the world we see each day. We can connect to our personal spirituality, and set it free so all can see the truth of our nature.

There is no time in truth, it always stays constant, but it grows in love. Love blossoms within us if we believe in ourselves. The new age is about reaching within and reconnecting to who you are. There are no judges, time limitations or special instructions. We have all we need to be what we dream about—a thing of beauty creating a world of love.

5. *Embraceable Me*

*When you embrace all the things about yourself that you find
unlovable, you have automatically allowed the space for its
opposite trait to manifest. Every action, every decision you
have has brought you to this place, this now. Bless all that has
happened in your life, which has been discordant. You have created
it all so you may know who you really are. Own it all. You are
not a victim, and neither is anyone else.*

Jani King is a New Zealand author who has written several
inspirational books. She explains that I create my world and all
I experience. That notion is hard to accept especially when it is
so easy to blame others for the mess I make around me. There is
always someone or something that I can yell at, be angry over or
hateful towards in order to cover my tracks. Those tactics seem
to work. Heck, everybody else does it. Not taking responsibility
for anything is a trait I see in others and I copy their behavior.
Life becomes what occurs while I am busy planning my future
and regretting my past in a cycle of not knowing who I am. Jani
says that is okay as long as I embrace these acts and realize that
I am not living in a state of love but drowning in the an ocean
of fear.

In order to understand this completely, I must throw the guilt,
hate, doubt, and self-pity in a boat of love and mark it OK. I must
look at myself as a work in progress and accept my hostile
actions as tools for growth. I must see them for what they
are—an ego driven quest to control everything and everybody
so I can feel whole. I want to feel whole and my lying is the road
to my truth.

Accepting all the things I've done through this lifetime is the
path of recovery. I open myself and allow the energy of life to
expand within me. Forgiveness is the lesson that keeps teaching

me and it is my quest to learn and practice it. The lesson begins with me and then I am able to express what I have learned. I feel room inside for more love and light and I bring it forth in gratitude. I become a whole— a sum of my parts connected to another whole which is the Divine Matrix of Love. In that matrix, there is nothing but pure peace. I can live in the now where the past is a part and the future is a part of what I am experiencing in this moment.

6. *Everything is Significant*

As the poet Rumi said, *"Wisdom is like the rain. Its source is limitless, but it comes down according to the season."*

Yes, I agree with that! As the seasons change, so does the wisdom. I am realizing that I am part of the wisdom that has been identified through all thoughts and actions recorded in time. The world, as I perceive it, is a different place than described by other minds through the centuries—different, but the same in significance. Everything is significant. Whether it is a world event or utensils in a drawer, each can connect or disconnect me to the awareness of who I am. My perceptions of events create my experience of them. All wisdom is within me to create my life as I believe it. Yep, I came equipped with all the wisdom to create an experience of remembering. We all did.

In the process of remembering, I go through a tunnel of time with portraits of people, events, and all types of gifts hanging on the walls: wisdom, talent and strength. It is my choice to pick who and what I want to experience. What wisdom do I want to be? What spirits do I want to go through the tunnel with? What gifts do I want to share? How strong shall I be? Each step is significant in the tunnel, and I am always able to change my direction. I can move forward, back, up, down, around, and out of the tunnel if I choose. For me, that's wisdom I began to remember.

My thoughts kept me in a place that had definite restrictions. I could only function in a certain manner because that's what wisdom said 50 years ago. My humanity was a hindrance to being whole. Part of my wisdom was tossed aside because it was insignificant at some point in my tunnel. I was only looking at the right side of the tunnel. The left side, the top, the bottom and the walls outside of the tunnel were insignificant. I was functioning according to someone else's wisdom, not mine. Of course the good news is, like the weather, I can change my wisdom. I can catch up with myself (my consciousness) in the tunnel. There is no right or wrong path to remembering. I'll get there at some point and it will be very significant.

We all travel through our life's tunnel at our own pace, some of us deeper in the tunnel than others. The beauty of our tunnels is we can always remember when we want to and be the significant wisdom enjoying ourselves with our source.

7. Exit and Enter Gracefully

Every exit is an entry somewhere else.

Tom Stoppard, the British playwright and screenplay writer of Brazil and Shakespeare in Love, said those words. Short but to the point, I do exit and enter different experiences all the time. My thoughts take me to the far reaches of my world. I enter another time, place and emotional reaction that becomes a new probability with unlimited choices. Once I exit that thought, I enter into another one that starts the process all over again.

I am constantly changing, exiting and entering different forms of consciousness. Unique aspects of myself blink on and off like a high speed pulsating light that catches the darkness with its awareness. I do this without trying and without the preconceived thought of blinking in and out of other realities. I am able to think and communicate without words or symbols. I feel the power of a connected energy running through me that propels me into daily expressions of life. I call it living—living in the now. This now brings me the pleasure of exiting one moment and entering another exciting one. The experience of life unfolds in a flash of consciousness.

The great German poet Rainer Maria Rilke explains this feeling of the now this way:

Later, he remembered certain moments in which the power of this moment was already contained, as in a seed. He thought of the hour in that other southern garden (Capri) when the call of a bird did not, so to speak, break off at the edge of his body, but was simultaneously outside and in his innermost being, uniting both into one uninterrupted space in which, mysteriously protected, only one single place of purest, deepest consciousness remained. On that occasion he had closed

*his eyes... and the infinite passed into him from all sides, so
intimately that he believed he could feel the stars which had in
the meantime appeared, gently reposing within his breast.*

The thrill of life is in the now—in the presence of the stars and
the all of nature that rests within me. I have unlimited energy
that brings me to the essence of being human, which is the
awareness of a greater now that is happening within me. I can
express it freely, exiting one thought and entering another
one gracefully.

8. Get on the Elephant

The word "enlightenment" seems to be the now age call for awareness—the awareness that I live in more than one consciousness at a time. I could think in more than one plane of existence at any given moment, but my focused consciousness is the one that I have learned to call "me." This "me" wanders around knowing there is more to it, but can't find the door that unlocks my other wonderful dimensions of thought. Searching for wholeness, I look to others to bring me to the place of unity where I think perfection rests.

I found this old Indian fable that illustrates the difficulty of holding the two conscious planes in mind simultaneously. When I look at them as one and the same, wisdom and foolishness are almost identical. They are indifferent to the world around them.

The story is about a young aspirant whose guru had just brought him to the realization that his essence is identical to the power that supports the universe, which we personify as "God." The youth, profoundly moved, exalted in the notion of himself as at one with the Lord and Being of the Universe, walked away in a state of profound absorption. When he had passed in that state through the village and onto the road beyond it, he beheld coming in his direction, a great elephant bearing a howdah on its back. The mahout, or driver, riding high on its neck above its head. The young candidate for sainthood was meditating on the proposition "I am God; All things are God." Upon perceiving the mighty elephant coming toward him, he added the obvious corollary, "The elephant is also God."

The animal, with its bells jingling to the majestic rhythm of its stately approach was steadily coming on, and the mahout above its head began shouting, "Clear the way! Clear the way, you idiot!"

The youth in his rapture was thinking still, "I am God; that elephant is God." Hearing the shouts of the mahout, he added, "Should God be afraid of God? Should God get out of the way of God?"

The phenomenon came steadily on with the driver at its head still shouting at him. The youth, in undistracted meditation, held both to his place on the road and to his transcendental insight until the moment of truth arrived. The elephant, simply wrapping its great trunk around the lunatic, tossed him aside, off the road.

Physically shocked, spiritually stunned, the youth landed all in a heap, not greatly bruised but altogether undone. Rising, not even adjusting his clothes, he returned, disordered, to his guru, to require an explanation. "You told me that I was God."

"Yes," said the guru, "you are God."

"You told me that all things are God. That elephant, then, was God?"

"So it was. That elephant was God. But why didn't you listen to the voice of God, shouting from the elephant's head to get out of the way?"

The moral of the story is that I am connected to the universal one of creation and that it is always guiding me through my emotions. When I ignore those emotions, I return to the focused state of consciousness that can distort my understanding of my physical journey. But somewhere inside of me is a mahout shouting, "Fool, get on the elephant and ride with me to another place that is filled with the wisdom of ALL THERE IS."

9. Earth Rocks

If we are to survive the accelerating changes that are coming our way, we need first to be flexible. We need to be able to let go of outdated assumptions and habits of thinking that no longer serve us. We need to find the inner freedom to see things with fresh eyes and respond more creatively. And second, we need greater inner stability. We need to be stably anchored in the ground of our own being, so that when we meet the unexpected we can remain cool, calm, and collected, not thrown into fear and panic.

Peter Russell is an author who holds degrees in theoretical physics and psychology from the University of Cambridge. He studied with Stephen Hawking while at Cambridge. He has a master's degree in computer science and has studied meditation and Eastern philosophy in India. Peter lectures businesses all over the world on self-development.

Change, the constant in our physical lives, seems to be more visible now than ever before. The news is filled with dramatic events that are reshaping our world: the fires in California, daily earthquakes across the globe, flooding from excessive rain and droughts from no rain. The ice is melting, the earth is warming and the seas are rising. No country or population is immune to the shifting poles as Mother Earth moves into another aspect of herself. Some say the blame rests with humans that squander, waste, neglect and abuse the natural elements that serve us in life. Perhaps we have contributed to our changing environment, but that has been our choice and from our choices many probabilities present themselves. We are living our choices and experiencing our thoughts.

As Peter points out, it is up to me to change along with my world in order to grow. Without change I stagnate, wither, and dry into a broken form that is void of energy. I move through these changes in fear and confusion worrying about me. I look for help and think I find it in unnecessary medications and senseless finger pointing. The problem is not me; it is everyone and everything I come in contact with including my friends and family.

Well, I can believe that and live in pain or I can learn how to live happily and freely in the face of change. My thoughts make that possible. Taking responsibility for myself mentally, physically and spiritually changes my beliefs.

Knowing that the earth is alive with consciousness and is moving into a new dimension of awareness is crucial in understanding what is happening in this present state of change. I am part of a new form of existence that is uniting me with myself. I am remembering other aspects of my consciousness that have been hidden by my ego mind. All of the changes are happening because I am observing them and experiencing life. They are visible now to help me not destroy myself. From these events, I am able to reconnect with my source of energy and change with it. Just like the tree in a storm, I must be flexible. I must be firmly rooted within myself. I must be accepting and resistance free.

The Age of Aquarius is now. It is an age with no age—only awareness of who I really am. I now remember I am a spirit having a human experience, here to express myself in love from the source of all love. I am ageless, timeless and filled with well-being. Now is my time to believe it!

10. Gnats against the Wind

You are under the power of no other enemy, are held in no other captivity, and want no other deliverance but from the power of your own earthly self. This is the murderer of the divine life within you. It is your own Cain that murders your own Abel.

William Law, an English mystic born in 1686, wrote those words. He was a follower of the works of Jacob Boehme—another European mystic, who was also a shoemaker.

While watching the events surrounding the death of a popular model unfold, I was reminded how true this statement can be. I will not go into detail for I'm sure you are aware that there is a struggle taking place concerning where she should be buried. Of course the underlying cause for the drama is money. There is a group of people in a bitter dispute over the physical remains of a person who is still very much alive in consciousness. Her experience of life now is out of the reach of money, anger, hatred and fear. But the group remaining is in their own "Hell" trying to make sense of the contrast they are creating. It's not about the dead; it's all about the grip of the earthly self on truth. Their own truth is being held captive by the allure of money. We do kill our brothers for the sake of an illusion. We kill ourselves for the sake of proving someone else wrong.

We asked a judge to tell us who is right so we can hide our feelings in justification. The judge had no better handle on his truth. He was lost like the defendants in the courtroom. It is entertainment for some, disgust for others and a non-event for the deceased.

I thought of a courtroom scene that Rumi wrote about over 700 years ago. It best describes my feelings. It's called, "Gnats against the Wind."

Some gnats come from the grass to speak to Solomon (the king). "O Solomon, you are the champion of the oppressed. You give justice to the little guys, and they don't get any littler than us. We are tiny metaphors for frailty. Can you defend us?"
"Who has mistreated you?" asked Solomon.

"Our complaint is against the wind."

"Well, said Solomon, you have pretty voices, you gnats, but remember a judge cannot listen to just one side, I must hear both litigants."

"Of course," Agree the gnats.

"Summon the east wind!" Solomon declares. And the wind arrives almost immediately.

"What happened to the gnat plaintiffs?" said Solomon.

Gone!

Such is the way of every seeker who comes to complain to the high court. When the presence of God arrives, where are the seekers? First there's dying, then union. Just like gnats inside the wind.

11. Yea, I Am In Awe!

Opportunities to find deeper powers within ourselves come when life seems most challenging. Negativism to the pain and ferocity of life is negativism to life. We are not there until we can say "yea" to it all. To take a righteous attitude toward anything is to denigrate it. Awe is what moves us forward.

Joseph Campbell was born in 1904. He was a professor, writer, orator and mythology expert. Joseph discovered that our lives and waking dreams are based on the myths we have learned and studied. The myths are the basis for many of our beliefs.

The belief in a deeper power within me has always been there. I never really understood what it was or did, so I recognized it from a distance and accepted my ignorance. I followed the path of others so I could solve my problems the way they did. I created my life and then wanted others to help me get out of it because the pain I experienced and fought against was winning. Instead of accepting and releasing the negative, I brought more of it to me by fighting against it and saying "no." As Joseph points out, the key is to say "yea" to all the things I manifest and work with them using allowance and forgiveness.

Being righteous and rigid are the ingredients that create fear. Awe is the spark that illuminates the deeper power within me. Gratitude is the vehicle that carries me through physical life, and laughter is the fuel that keeps me going to that place of power where I am able to express love for all the diversity around me. "Yea" with a smile and the power within me brings me to that place I never left; I just ignored it.

Campbell continues, *"As you proceed through life, following your own path, birds will shit on you. Don't bother to brush it off. Getting a comedic view of your situation gives you spiritual distance. Having a sense of humor saves you."*

Now is the time for awareness. Now is the only time I experience. Now is the time to laugh at myself and smile in awe. Now is the time to be who I am and enjoy my journey. Now is the time for love.

12. Time to Pop the Lid off the Box

The moon's the same old moon, the flowers exactly as they were,
yet I've become the thingness of all the things I see!

That is the 17th century (1602-76) Japanese poet Bunan
explaining a very important element of who we are. How I see
myself is a very important part of how I see the world around me.

It is so easy for me, in this 3-D world of time and space, to
see everything in black and white. I can add a little color now
and then but for the most part, I have cut an image of
myself out of thought while moving through my daily life.
Sometimes I'm comfortable with it, other times it seems like
it's not me. Everything around me stays the same, but I feel
different. Another me? Could very well be.

Through discoveries in science, I now know that atoms work in
amazing ways. They actually pulsate in patterns and rhythms.
My mind works the same way. What I focus my attention on
is what I experience. So, I could walk down the same street
everyday and see the same thing and miss many other events
that are happening on that street. I could see the same people
daily because that's who I look for. I am seeing and feeling what
I taught myself to experience. But there is so much right before
me that I miss because I believe that what I see is all there is.
I am in the box of my own thoughts with the lid closed.

Bunan, in his ancient wisdom, opened the lid and crawled out of
the box. He awakened his mind with his consciousness and saw
a new life. He saw a connection with all he experienced.
He was not separated in thought from his surroundings,

but he was united in consciousness. He felt himself, instead of seeing himself. Feelings are the language of the universe. Bunan could communicate with all of it because he knew he was it. His beginning had no ending. It was united with ALL THERE IS.

I am no different than Bunan. I am a connected consciousness waiting to discover other aspects of myself when I decide to get out of my box. I look around and see the same things, but I feel differently about them. Then, I start to see new things, I am able to feel people for who they are instead of painting a judgmental picture. I can feel my home, work, and activities with new energy because I express myself in love. I become this "thingness" of everything by changing my thoughts about who I am.

I am just now realizing what I have intuitively known forever. I am consciousness connected to all things in a web of love attached to a divine matrix of ALL THERE IS. With that knowledge, my life has no age or limitations unless I crawl back into the box.

Growth

1. A Cinder of Unity

If the cloth had its own fixed, unchangeable self-essence, it could not be made from the thread... the cloth comes from the thread and the thread from flax... It is just like the ... burning and the burned. They are brought together under certain conditions, and thus there takes place a phenomenon called burning... each has no reality of its own. For when one is absent the other is put out of existence. It is so with all things in this world, they are empty, without self, without absolute existence. They are like the will-o'-the-wisp.

That statement comes from the ancient Indian King and philosopher, Pingalaka. Some say he lived 200 years after Buddha's death. Although I have not read very much about him or his work, his words strike a note of remembering within me.

So much written information in many different languages has become available to us over the years. Thanks to the Internet, I am now able to read and remember some of the innate knowledge I have within me. When I could only learn what was written in English, I was restricted in what I understood about myself. I was caught in a world of partial knowledge and believed that I, the cloth, was a reality on its own. I did not think about the other aspects of myself that make me who I am. Without the match and the wood working together, I cannot burn. I am the wood without the match when focusing only on the physical aspect. As Pinglaka points out, I am an illusion, walking in a fog of forgetfulness, waiting to wake up.

So it is, I can walk through physical life disconnected, searching for answers, or I can look within myself and discover the world I left behind. My mirror is there, burning in the flame of love. All the illusions turn to ashes and I am a cinder of unity. Loneliness is not a thought, or a word. Everything is there, around my fire of truth. I am who I am, seeing myself in many realities. Living in the cycle of eternity connected to ALL THERE IS, Love.

2. A Flowering Universe

Simple thoughts manifest into wonderful actions. I found a few thoughts to share today; each message resonates in unity. Unity starts within me and then spreads through my world, carried by the winds of gratitude and peace. I become a flowering universe blooming in a multidimensional reality that produces seeds of abundance from eternal roots of awareness. My roots are connected to a stream of consciousness that waters me with infinite love. All things do move in me, through me, and I express myself in the oneness of ALL THERE IS.

To be simple is a blessing; to be holy is to live knowing I am simple; simplicity is freedom; freedom is the essence of creation.

May all things move in me
and know and be known in me
May all creation
dance for joy within me.

~Chinook Psalter

Just to be is a blessing
Just to live is holy

~Rabbi Abraham Heschel

When I rise up
let me rise up joyful
like a bird
When I fall
let me fall without regret
like a leaf

~Wendell Berry

Earth brings us into life
and nourishes us
Earth takes us back again
Birth and death are present in every moment

~Thich Nhat Hanh

All are nothing but flowers
In a flowering universe.

~Nakagawa Soen-Roshi

Watching gardeners label their plants
I vow with all beings
to practice the old horticulture
and let the plants identify me.

~Robert Aitken

From all that dwells below the skies
Let faith and hope with joy arise,
Let beauty, truth and good be sung
Through every land, by every tongue.

~Unitarian Prayer

3. A Seed of Change

The nature of the universe loves nothing so much as to change things which are and to make new things like them. For everything that exists is in a manner the seed of that which will be.

Marcus Aurelius was born in 121 AD. He was the Roman Emperor from 161 to 180. He is considered an important stoic philosopher. His work, The Meditations, has been praised for its exquisite accent and its infinite tenderness. Marcus understood that change is the only constant we experience.

It's certainly not difficult to see how change defines my life; I am, as Marcus explains, a seed of that which will be. Just like a seed, I expand and express myself in physical form. I change shapes and size; I grow internally and externally. My appearance shifts and flows with my surroundings. I am like the seed; a root, a branch, a leaf, a trunk, constantly adjusting to the element of time and the illusion of space. Planted firmly in the now, I can experience changes and alter my thinking to enjoy them. The beauty of an old tree is just as special as the young one, each with purpose and desire. Accepting the lessons of change, my roots of love grow and connect to roots of fulfillment. I become the physical expression of universal consciousness that is constantly expanding and changing.

Change is infinite growth; it is acceptance. Where it starts and where it goes is always flowing into the stream of consciousness. That stream is the foundation of life, not only my physical life, but my spiritual one as well. It is the form of everything and the shape of nothing. It is gentle, kind, brutal and cunning, depending on my thoughts about it. It is my best teacher and my worst nightmare. I make change real by creating it in my world. All I have to do is name it and live it.

So here I am—a work in progress, filled with questions, and searching for answers that are locked in change. My journey is to remember where I put the key that unlocks the door of change. I look everywhere and in everything, and continue to evolve without knowing who I am. When I stop looking and allow myself to open like the seed, I change again. I become what I have been fighting. I forgive myself and live. I become aware of other aspects of myself and I welcome the unity. My emotions set me free and I expand in the web of awareness and connection. I am no longer one seed, but many—each one desiring to be a grander version of the tree of life.

No longer alone, I move like the wind and dance to the music of love. The nature of my nature is change, and in that world, I am free.

4. A Smile, a Kiss and a Heart Filled with Gratitude

Misery is optional.

How easy it is to forget that, especially when I experience something or someone that makes me uncomfortable. I immediately blame my dis-ease on everything but myself; I take no responsibility for the thoughts that create my pain. Overlooking my creations, I see a world locked in turmoil. Once separated from my true feelings, I become the poster child for misery, and the catalyst for a stress-filled life.

Well, you know what comes next, more of the same thing, unpleasant thoughts that manifest into negative words and actions. I attract all the agony that goes with unhappiness, guilt and anger. My world is a melting pot of fear, hate and enemies. My mind is trapped in a well of paranoia, where everything is out to get me.

Okay, so what's the solution? How can I get out of this life of separation? Change is the pill. Changing my thoughts creates new words and actions. My desire to feel better and to ask for help from my source of energy will work miracles.

I am energy connected to a web of energy that is the foundation for all life. That foundation is consciousness and exists in all matter. It is there to assist me through this physical journey not through pain, but in joy. My awareness of this consciousness is the change I need to redirect my life. It will guide me through my feelings and emotions and I will vibrate in the stream of positivity that is this consciousness.

It only takes a thought to change my world; the thought of unity within myself is the miracle I have been waiting to see. If I believe that I am a whole part of another whole that is the essence of love, then I will experience that belief.

Then, I express that belief through my words and actions. By expressing that thought, I become what the whole is—love manifested physically. I grow and expand in the process of change.

I am love and there is no room for anything else. Love is ALL THERE IS. Someone said, *"The holiest place on earth is where ancient hatred has become a present love."* That place is within me. In order to love my world, I must love myself; I must forgive myself and walk down my path with a smile, a kiss and a heart filled with gratitude. Abundance surrounds me in peace and I become a grander version of who I am.

5. A Stage of Fools

*'That happiness endures which comes from the grinding together
of anguish and ecstasy and from the intensity of the grinding.
That knowledge is true which comes from the searching into
doubts and beliefs and from the depth of searching.*

An anonymous sage wrote that during the Ming Dynasty.
It explains the contrast we experience on our journey and how
it turns into happiness as we face it and work through it.
From anguish comes ecstasy and none too soon I might add,
for pain of any kind is difficult for us to understand.

So many poets and writers have expressed this unavoidable
feeling. Rumi said, *"The cure for pain is the pain. Good and
bad are mixed. If you don't have both, you don't belong to us."*

And, William Blake penned:

*Joy and woe are woven fine,
A clothing for the soul divine.
Under every grief and pine
Runs a joy with silken twine.*

And, then there are these Shakespeare lines from King Lear:

*Thou must be patient; we came crying hither: Thou know'st the
first time that we smell the air, we wail and cry... When we are
born, we cry that we are come to this great stage of fools.*

From the contrast, I grow. If I had nothing but sameness on my
journey, I would stay the same. It is the contrast and the lessons
learned that reconnect me to who I am. Each pain is a step in the

process of remembering. Each hurt is a badge of understanding. All put before me, by me, to expand and become a grander version of myself.

I experience just one aspect of myself in physical form. I have many selves that interact with the consciousness I call me. I can feel another me through pain. I can face the drama in life with no mask but my truth. I can be and grow in gratitude without fear, knowing the lessons are worth the anguish. If I believe in the freedom of free will and become aware of the messages that are put before me, I can reconnect to all life, and bless the contrast.

From the darkness comes light. I don't have to force it, it just comes. Becoming is the nature of all life, and the gift I give myself.

Am I a crying fool on this stage of life? Or, am I a spirit experiencing just one aspect of ALL THERE IS, Love?

6. Circles on Water

*I go among trees and sit still. All my stirring becomes quiet
around me like circles on water. My tasks lie in their places
where I left them, asleep like cattle. Then, what is afraid of me
comes and lives a while in my sight. What it fears in me leaves
me, and the fear of me leaves it. It sings and I hear its song.
Then, what I am afraid of comes. I live for a while in its sight.
What I fear in it leaves it, and the fear of it leaves me. It sings
and I hear its song.*

Wendell Berry was born in 1934 and is a prolific author of novels,
short stories, poems and essays. He taught at the University of
Kentucky in the late 1980's and early 1990's, and he now farms,
resides and writes at Lane's Landing, his farm near Port
Royal, Kentucky.

Sitting quietly among the trees is a wonderful experience.
Surrounded by their grace and beauty they bring peace to a
racing mind. The trees stand rooted in a consciousness that
express love of creation and the joyful expansion of being. I have
learned to appreciate their silent qualities and abundant love.
I can relate to Wendell's words; many things have come to me
and stood before me while I sit with my friends, the trees.

Fear likes to play with me. It grabs my mind and squeezes my
thoughts, so that all I feel is a tight knot of pain. Every idea,
every notion becomes a minefield of doubt. I wrestle with myself
trying to untie the knot, but it tightens as I struggle. My world
fills with anger, distrust and hate, and I express those emotions.
I create an illusion of mystery in order to hide from my feelings.
I lie to myself and the world as perceive it is filled with monsters.
All of my energy is drained from the battle that is raging within me.
I am a square knot in the smooth rope of life.

As Berry discovered, nature holds the answer to untangling my thoughts. It is a connected part of me. It sits waiting for me to wake up and begin to live. My thoughts of separation have taken me away from the unity that surrounds me and I walk in circles, like the circles on water.

I realize what I do to myself. I know I create my reality by my thoughts. I know my choices become the probabilities I experience. I can and do change by asking for help. I am part of a universal consciousness that is filled with nothing but love. I can fill my body and mind with its energy and release myself from the knots of fear and despair. That is what nature does in its own reality as it expands in awareness.

By accepting, releasing and forgiving the fear, I become a grander version of who I am. I am one with nature and with ALL THERE IS in a web of consciousness that expands and grows in the infinite field of love.

7. *From My World to Yours*

I know that nothing has ever been real without my beholding it. All becoming has needed me. My looking ripens things and they come toward me, to meet and be met.

Ranier Maria Rilke's poem from the book, "Love Poems to God", tells me that I play an important part in how my life unfolds physically. Just by looking at something or someone they change. Quantum physics explains that is exactly what happens to atoms and molecules when attention is given to them, they change. My thoughts are much stronger than what I have been taught to understand, for they shape the world where I exist.

We are all connected in a web of love, and it is very apparent that we all are different within the web. It seems like we live in our own world, connected to the world around us, but separated by our individual thoughts. Within my own world, I can change how I view the other worlds, and they in turn change. Each thought creates energy that spews outward and manifests itself in some way, a word, or action, or a silent message that is understood without words. From the matter I created, I live day to day believing in what I have become. In this creation I am united with my creator, in an inner marriage of love. That union is always present, but sometimes forgotten, by the choices I make in my world. It's not measured in good or bad, but in growth and learning—the very reason I experience my world.

By simply changing my thoughts I change so many things around me. I will never know how my thoughts affect this change unless I become aware of the power that rests within me. It can be used to create a heaven or a hell, and I can bring others with me, if they allow it. I can feel brightness in the dark and see darkness in the light. It's my world, my choice. I want to grow and learn to be the grander version of myself, united with my whole being, and share that feeling with the rest of the worlds that mirror mine.

I am what I believe and I believe I am love. My world loves all worlds united in ALL THERE IS, Love.

8. Gaps of Silence

The gaps are the thing. The gaps are the spirit's one home, the altitudes and latitudes so dazzling spare and clean that the spirit can discover itself like a once-blind man unbound. The gaps are the clefts in the rock where you cower to see the back parts of God; they are the fissures between mountains and cells; the wind lances through the icy narrowing fiord's splitting the cliffs of mystery. Go up into the gaps. If you can find them; they shift and vanish too. Stalk the gaps. Squeak into a gap in the soil, turn and unlock—more than a maple—a universe.

Annie Dillard was born in Pittsburgh, Pennsylvania in 1945. She is a writer and poet. She won the Pulitzer Prize in 1975 for her work *Pilgrim at Tinker Creek*. That work was written after she survived an almost fatal attack of pneumonia.

Annie remembered her spirit by using nature as an analogy. The above quote describes her reunion, and she gives me a road map to rediscover mine. I can feel the gaps within me and remember who I am. The gaps within me are the road signs of remembering.

The rocks I place in my path of remembering through distorted beliefs and thoughts hide my spirit. I must move those rocks and see what waits beneath them in the gaps of thought. The mountains of fear and anger and the winds of verbal abuse, hide my spirit. I must climb the mountains, embrace the fear and swallow the wind in order to feel my true self, in the gap of freedom. The frozen emotions of hate and judgment cover my spirit. I must melt these icy thoughts in forgiveness so that my spirit can surface through the gap of physical life.

By searching within myself, leaving no stones of ego unturned, unlocking the doors of the past and releasing them in love, I remember the gaps—the gaps where my spirit waits—the gaps of remembering who I am. There is silence in the gaps. A silence filled with love.

I feel the silence and touch a part of me that has been hidden in illusion. I can become the silence at anytime; that is my choice. My beliefs create the gaps. I can express myself fully by being silent. I can expand and grow into a grander version of physical form.

The gaps are my store of silence. No purchase required. Peace, abundance and joy are free there, and the inventory never goes out of stock.

9. Girl in Love

Rainer Maria Rilke was born in Prague in 1875. The master poet of Modernism in the German-speaking world lived most of his life in self-imposed exile traveling across Europe. He was an artist, a poet's poet, whose work is unsurpassed in its sense of mastery and consummate craftsmanship.

Rilke was one of the first poets I studied when I began my quest to remember who I am. His work filled me with the desire to express myself in some way, so I began to write again. Thanks to him and Rumi, along with several others, I woke up from the dream that I call reality and discovered different worlds that exist simultaneously. This awakening continues and the expansion of thought that it offers is pure magic; it's a mystery with no end. Each minute is a window that opens to another experience.

Rilke's poem "Girl in Love," written in the early 1900's, expresses his sense of what the mystery holds within it. He feels another aspect of himself and begins to remember what it is. As Rilke says, "I have space to spare inside of me," and now is the time to fill it with love. Disappearing in love is the act of complete surrender; it is the art of self-creation.

Girl in Love

That's my window. This minute
So gently did I alight
From sleep-was still floating in it.
Where has my life its limit
And where begins the night?

I could fancy all things around me
Where nothing but I as yet;
Like a crystal's depth, profoundly
Mute, translucent, unlit.

I have space to spare inside me
For the stars, too: so full of room
Feels my heart; so lightly
Would it let go of him, whom

For all I know I have started
To love, it may be to hold.
Strange, as if never charted,
Stares my fortune untold.

Why is it I am bedded
Beneath this infinitude,
Fragrant like a meadow,
Hither and thither moved,

Calling out, yet fearing
Someone might hear the cry,
Destined to disappearing
Within another I.

10. How's my Garden Grow?

Each portion of matter may be conceived of as a garden full of plants, and a pond full of fishes. But each branch of the plant, each member of the animal, each drop of its humors, is also such a garden or such a pond.

Gottfried Leibriz was born in 1646. He was educated in law and philosophy, and he played an important role in politics and mathematics in the 17th century. He invented calculus and his notation is in general use today. He discovered the binary system, which is the foundation of all modern computer architectures. He, along with Descartes and Spinoza, are considered the greatest rationalists of the 17th century.

Leibriz knew that there was more to matter than meets my eyes. He was able to understand that this significant otherness that was contained in matter was energy. Each inanimate object was composed of energy, no matter what name we assigned to it. All are works of beauty, and all contained a world within themselves.

Quantum physics has defined me now, by using the term "energy." I am energy that is fueled by another energy that has still not been given an exact name. Of course there are many names for it: God, the Universe, the Source, the One, the All. This energy, I call love, is in everything and manifests itself in different ways. It connects all living things in its web and expands in each physical entity. My consciousness, spirit, body and mind are examples of how this energy grows. When I am fully connected to this energy and aware of it, my world expands through my thoughts and beliefs. I am a garden just as Leibriz describes, filled with beauty. I need nothing more than this positive flow of infinity to feel who I am. I live to learn and remember. I see my world as heaven—the heaven that I thought was a mystery.

Without it, or by blocking it with my thoughts, I experience the hell I fear so much. I am weak, scared, and lonely. Distortion rules my life. My garden becomes filled with weeds, and slowly I die, thus creating the death I always feared. My life is not a life, but a world of pain, suffering, and anger. I look everywhere for relief, except the one place where it waits, within me.

Gottfried had the right idea. Everything is a beautiful garden. All I need to do is feel it, experience it, and express gratitude for my awareness. If I feel the beauty within me, I will manifest beauty. All life and all physical objects have beautiful energy running through them. Each there for me to learn and grow into a grander version of the garden I call Hal. I am the energy of love.

11. Trust Would Settle Every Problem Now

A Course in Miracles reminds me that the simple act of trusting makes my life a wonderful journey. Trust is something that is innately present in all of us.

As a child, I had no problem trusting my parents, or the church, or my country; they all were figures of strength, honesty and love in my eyes. I felt a great sense of well-being knowing I could go about my daily acts of having fun in complete freedom. My world was filled with everything I needed to be a happy human.

Then, something happened, I'm not sure when, but I started to lose trust; it left me holding fear in one hand and anger in the other. My world went from a haven of acceptance to a den of misgivings. This dramatic change in my thinking altered my view of the world around me. I became a misfit, unable to believe anything, including myself. I lost my identity, and found pseudo relief in mimicking the acts of others. I was an empty shell, like a confused hermit crab moving from place to place. I lived in a world of lies, each lie sinking me deeper in the sand of sickness. Helpless, I sank into a puddle of depression.

Several years later I read the book, *Ask and it is Given*, written by Ester and Jerry Hicks and my trust returned. It never was lost; it was forgotten through years of external conditioning. I had to remember how to trust myself in order to gain that childhood feeling again. I had to ask for help from my source and then trust that it would come by allowing the energy of life to flow through me. I offered no resistance. I believed that something inside me would change what I had experienced through mistrust. My thoughts vibrated in love and I accepted love with gratitude. I started to feel with my emotions and always found the better thought.

Gradually I started to trust myself again, and this feeling of wellness filled my body and mind. I found myself trusting others and believing in the innate beauty we all have within us. My world reversed its poles and I was released from the puddle of depression. I reconnected to my source of energy and began to live again.

Trust does settle every problem. By trusting myself, I can set an example and allow that trust to touch those around me. Trust is truth and it always rests in freedom. By being aware of the power I have within me, I can be the child who lives in a world that accepts problems and releases them in the arms of trust.

12. Okay, I Accept Myself!

The most terrifying thing is to accept oneself completely.

Carl Jung, the founder of analytical psychology, was born
in 1875. His work has influenced the thinking process of all of
us in one way or another. He emphasized balance and harmony
in everyday life, not relying too much on science and logic
but integrating a mix of spiritually and appreciation for the
unconscious realms of ourselves.

Getting to accept myself for what I am is a never ending quest.
I seem to change constantly and without notice. One minute I
am filled with excitement and the next minute filled with rage.
Controlling my emotions is an ongoing work and expressing
them honestly is a difficult task. I find myself searching for the
right action in wrong situations and end up confused by my
judgmental mind. Each roadblock I encounter in life becomes
a pothole of fear and my vehicle falls apart along the way.
As Jung points out I am terrified to accept the complete me,
because I am too busy with the half of me that is unraveling in
day-to-day experiences. I try to figure out my state of mind with
the same mind that created the mayhem. All the while there
is another part of me sitting on the sidelines of consciousness
waiting for the frazzled me to recognize its power.

Giving my power to something other than a tangible entity
is very difficult. I have been trained to be in control of my
destiny and stay the course in a state of confusion even if it
is a detriment to wellness. Through my education, I learned
that my abilities are limited and that external remedies would
comfort me; science and logic reign supreme and I needed to
be in agreement with them in order to be whole. Jung thought
differently and he tapped into other aspects of his consciousness
to solve his problems. He was aware of his inner world of authenticity.

Jung wrote about the fear of knowing "self" completely. That awareness changes everything I learned about my external world. Uniting with the internal source of all energy brings new thoughts, new experiences and new expressions to my physical existence. Connecting to the consciousness that is a stream of love removes the terror and anguish from my old thoughts and I feel a new me. I accept who I am, and create a world of peace, abundance, and love. I act in gratitude, and share my wealth with all life. I walk in honest shoes and dress in fearless clothes. My head is filled with dreams of adventure and discovery. My body is balanced by freedom and change.

I looked into the abyss that is within me and found it looking back at me with eyes of love. The object and the subject are now one—growing and expanding into a grander version of a spirit having a human experience.

Gateway

1. A Flowing Silence

The wonderful story of Jelaluddin Rumi and the Shams of Tabriz told by Coleman Barks is a true love story. It happened in Turkey over 700 years ago, and I knew nothing about it until 1996, the year Mother passed. I was drawn to the beauty of their ancient relationship and how they expressed it. The story itself seemed mythical but real, and I felt a deep sense of understanding when I read it for the first time. Rumi's poetry became a focal point in my life and I changed my opinion of who I was by reading his words.

There are several different versions of how Rumi and Shams met, but most agree that it happened in 1244 while Rumi was teaching some of his students and reading from one of his father's books. Rumi's family members were teachers and scholars at that time, and had a group of followers in the village of Konya, Turkey. Although he was not from that village, Shams was in that group that day. He broke through the group and grabbed the book from Rumi along with the other books Rumi had with him, and threw them into a nearby pool of water.

"What are you and what are you doing?" asks Rumi.

"It is time for you to live what you've been reading," replied Shams.

Rumi turns to the books in the water.

"We can retrieve them, if that's what you want," Shams says. "They will be perfectly dry, just as they were." Shams lifts one out to show him. It was dry.

"Let them stay," Rumi responded.

Those books were a rare, complex entity back in the thirteenth century, giving them up was a deep act of surrendering. So this was the start of a friendship that became a way. There is a break between words in books and sacred experiences. Rumi had to go deeper, and by abandoning his books he understood that words and language are not living. Rumi says that over and over again in his poetry.

Rumi and Shams went off into month long periods of what is called "sohbet," or twin novas of conversational dance that had tremendous creative energy within it; a force field of crackling energy. They blended so well they created a new mysticism. They found in each other the indescribable third script, which cannot be understood by mind but only known as its presence is felt.

Shams said, "The writing comes in three scripts. One that I, and only I, can read; one that I and others can read; and one that neither I nor anyone else can read. I am that third script." The Konya community felt jealous of this friendship between Rumi and Shams. They plotted to force Shams away and eventually killed him and hid his body. Rumi searched for Shams everywhere until one day he realized Shams was within him. There was no need to search anymore; Rumi was the essence of the friendship. With that knowledge he began speaking and writing poetry that is now loved and embraced by everyone around the world.

That story had a major impact on my life. Rumi's own loss made me realize where my mother had gone. She never left me; she was within me and her love for me was stronger than it had ever been in physical form. I found her love and my feelings of loss turned into expressions of gratitude. My writing is an example of unity; an example of truth; an example of the faith that I found within me. I share it with the same act of love that Rumi taught me. I share it with love from my mother.

I found this poem, "Autumn Rose Elegy," in Coleman Barks book, *The Glance.*

You've gone to the secret world.
Which way is it?
You broke the cage and flew.
You heard the drum that calls you home.
You left this humiliating shelf,
This disorienting desert
Where we're given wrong directions.
What use now a crown?
You've become the sun.
No need for a belt:
You've slipped out of your waist!
I have heard that near the end
You were eyes looking at soul.
No looking now.
You live inside the soul.
You're the strange autumn rose
That led the winter wind in
By withering.
You're rain soaking everywhere
From cloud to ground.
No bother of talking.
Flowing silence and sweet sleep
Beside the friend.

2. Theory of What?

We must close our eyes and invoke a new manner of seeing... a
wakefulness that is the birthright of us all, though few put it to use.

Those words from Plotinus, a Greek philosopher born in the
year 205, tell us something about ourselves that we all know.
William James, the twentieth century philosopher, said it this
way: *"Most people live, whether physically, intellectually or*
morality, in a very restricted circle of their potential being.
They make use of a very small portion of their possible
consciousness."

There is more to me than meets the eye. More than science has
been able to identify at this point in time. An awakening of
consciousness is changing who we think we are. The world as
we know it is becoming a place where we can unite thoughts
given to us through the centuries and live an integral way of life.
Rather than segregating thoughts from different religions,
politics, spiritual paths, we can now approach consciousness as
being connected and blend thoughts into a universal mode
of knowing. We have all the tools available to do it, we need to
use them.

It is not a quick solution unless I believe it is. I must start the
change within myself. By doing that, I begin to change my world
and it becomes reality. When I feel connected to all life, there
is another aspect of myself that lives physically. I bring the past
and the future into my now, and live in unity. I can start to feel
who I am, and then I change what I look like and what I see.

Ken Wilbur, one of our modern day philosophers, calls it
"Integral Psychology or the Theory of Everything," and he
has developed it into an understandable approach to living in
the twenty-first century. He has spent years trying to bring

the science, religion, politics, and spirituality into a flowing stream of connected information that empties into the sea of collective consciousness. By understanding our connection and appreciating diversity, we can solve many of the problems that we face each day. As Ken said:

I believe that integral psychology and integral studies in general, will become prevalent in the coming decades, as the academic world gropes it way out of its doggedly night view of the Kosmos.

Ken's ideas are being studied all over the world. He now has a University dedicated to teaching the integral approach in science, business, politics and religion. I believe in unity without restrictions. I think we all do.

3. Am I Dreaming Or What?

*In a dream, I saw myself as a great butterfly with wings that
spanned all of creation; now I am not sure if I was Chuang-Tsu
dreaming I was a butterfly, or if I am a butterfly dreaming I
am Chuang-Tsu.*

Those are the words of the Chinese Patriarch Chuang-Tsu. You
know he's got a point. What is the deal with this dual life I live?
About half of the day while awake, I see a world around me with
my eyes wide open. When I go to sleep, my eyes are closed and
I see and experience another world that takes me on adventures
in consciousness. I see, touch, and live in another density.
Which one is real? Maybe they are both real. I am creating both
of them.

The scientists say that I create these dreams from fragments of
unresolved situations in my life, or latent desires or even past
life experiences. Okay, that might make sense. But, one thing
is for sure, I create them and they can be very real. They can
be revealing, exciting, adventurous and fearful. I see friends,
animals, all sorts of wild situations, and even departed souls
whom I have known. I visit places I never knew about, I fly
without wings or planes. I laugh, I cry, I love. I do all this and
never leave the comfort of my bed. While dreaming, there
is no other time, only dreamtime. I am living in a different
reality—reality meaning the fact of being true to life.

Indigenous people around the globe speak of the "Now Time"
which they experience daily and the "Dream Time" which
existed before the "Now Time." This belief has continued
through ages in different forms; religious beliefs and other cult
formats call it heaven and hell. We all have been exposed to a
belief in another reality. It is our choice to believe or not.

I have more than one self. I have the consciousness who is writing this note fully awake, both feet on the floor, and I have another self who needs no body to experience different events and express innate desires. All I need is my consciousness that never sleeps. While my daytime consciousness sleeps, in order to heal the physical body, I am free to travel to points within myself that I forgot existed. Understanding that I can use my dream world to connect to another reality, experience myself in another form and heal myself makes this event exciting.

Remember, what you believe, you will experience, and then you will express that belief and then become the belief. With multidimensional thought, I open my mind to the universe and to ALL THAT IS.

4. Break Time

*Most people have a hard time delegating, or even wanting
to delegate, because you have been justifying your existence
through hard work, and you equate success with struggle; you
equate results with struggle. And so, you sort of wear your
struggle like a badge of honor. That is opposite of allowing
the Well-being. The only thing that ever matters in success
or achievement is your achieving the things that you want to
achieve. So, if you are setting standards and you're feeling
uncomfortable about the standards that you've set, tweak the
standards back a little bit. Ratchet it back a notch. Give yourself
a break. Give yourself the benefit of the doubt. Lighten up. Be easier.
Go slower. Take it easy. Have more fun. Love yourself more.
Laugh more. Appreciate more. All is well. You can't get it wrong.
You never get it done.*

Those words are from Ester Hicks author of the book, *Ask and
it is Given.* What a nice way to start the day, I can free myself
of the struggle and aggravation I put myself through daily. I can
look at myself with new eyes and realize I am the one who adds
the stress factor in my life by struggling against everything I
encounter in this physical world. Instead of creating problems, I
can create a life without the badge of struggle. After all, what
is important: my well-being or worrying about the pile of
insecurity that I have labeled as success? The only one keeping
score is me. There is no power greater than love and I am filled
with it. However, I have buried it under the sea of self-doubt
and fear. Ester tells me how to find it again.

How can I laugh in the face of misery? How can I relax when
I have bills to pay? How can I have fun when my job is full of
frustration? Ester makes it sound so easy. She says to let go and
allow the energy of love to take over; trust in myself and accept
where I am now; release the anger and pain by having fun and by

thinking thoughts that make me smile. I'll do whatever makes me happy. I know I am guided by the power of love. Struggle is a state of mind and I can change that through my thoughts. I don't need a badge to prove anything to anyone. All I need is within me. It is called my freedom to choose. I have the ability to fight and resist my daily tasks, or I can accept and allow them with my thoughts of appreciation.

Any contrast I encounter in daily life is there for a reason. It is a lesson, dressed as a challenge, and it is there for me to learn something. I grow from the contrast when I accept it and move through it without resistance. I have many choices from all the probabilities that surround me every minute. Whatever my choice, it is okay for me to experience it. From that choice, another one will surface and I will continue on my journey choosing and experiencing and expressing myself. Each choice is called living. How easy it is to choose the thoughts that make me feel full of love, instead of forcing myself to live in untruthfulness.

Ester says be free, relax, enjoy, laugh, and appreciate who I am. Appreciate all I have and all those who surround me on my journey of remembering. By giving myself a break I can become the spirit that is free to be whatever I choose. I can achieve and not struggle. I can be a success in my own eyes and express that feeling in gratitude. When I realize that love is the essence of my life, I will also realize that no matter what I do, I can never get it wrong and I will never get it done. Then my world becomes a place of peace and joy. I am connected to the stream of well-being that flows from the source of ALL THERE IS.

5. Day Dream Believer

*Look, look, look to the rainbow. Follow it over the hill and the
stream. Look, look, look to the rainbow. Follow the fellow who
follows his dream.*

That's from the wonderful play Finnian's Rainbow, which hit
Broadway in 1947. The poem has an interesting point about
looking to the rainbow within myself. I am trying to do that
more each day.

There has always been something mystical about daydreaming.
I know some religious groups frown upon it saying, "Idle minds
are the workshops of the devil." I'm not sure when that mentality
started, but I don't buy it.

I have had some great visions of myself and my world, by simply
taking myself to another place via my thoughts—especially
when the physically situation I was in didn't suit me for one
reason or another. I know it can be rude to do that, especially
when in a group, but to be honest some of my greatest
daydreams came about when I should have been focused on
some event others thought was important. Of course, I always
return to face the music when I hear someone say, "You weren't
even listening, Hal. Where were you, on some beach with
an illusion?" Well maybe I was, and it sure felt good!

Just like my sleep dreams, my daydreams are filled with
important messages from my psyche, if I take the hint and try
to understand them. After all, I am creating them, and there is
something in them I should connect with. It may be that I need
to adjust my normal way of putting everything in time and space,

and let my consciousness run wild. That takes some practice but no doubt the benefits are worth the exercise. I begin to know more about the real me that I have been searching for. There I am, right where I left myself. Amazing!

By releasing myself from beliefs of unworthiness brought about by distorted educational systems, I can begin to free a part of me and unite with other parts of myself. This reunion brings new awareness to the word "life." It adds color to a flat canvas of thought. I paint myself with vibrant shades of energy, and I no longer confine myself to a three-dimensional world. I recognize that there is more to me than I was taught. I start to feel my way through daily events, rather than suffer through them. I open my belief system to include thoughts I have suppressed, because I was told it was not the right way to live. I take back my right to co-create my life and expand in my expression of love.

I am a daydream believer, who just wrote this excerpt by believing it was already written. With good intentions, imagination, and by following my impulses, Love surrounds me. That's the dream I'll have every day and I don't want to wake up!

6. Death by Design?

Death is different living for the exalted one. His soul becomes
calm and settled. Death is union, not torture and suffering.
It's different than the ignorant one who dies all the time.

Once again my friend, Rumi, says so much in so few words.
Death, the biggest fear for most of us, is not really a big deal
unless we make it that way through ignorance.

Scientifically speaking the cells and molecules within my body
are dying and being reborn all the time. The body I had ten
years ago was filled with different cells and molecules than
what are present today. The old cells died, but my physical form
remained. My consciousness stayed focused on my physical self,
and I continued to "live," but I changed, grew and expanded over
those ten years. I experienced death within myself, but I was
not aware of it, because I hid that part from myself. No need to
understand how my body works, it just works, right?

If I am capable of hiding that experience from myself, what else
can I hide? It turns out pretty much anything can be locked
away in a cell or group of cells waiting to die or be released.
This will bring about the death of my physical form sooner than
I expected, but it is a choice I make consciously. If I choose to, I
can believe that I do it subconsciously, but I am still making
the choice. I can blame it on someone or something else.
There are plenty of things available to make me think I am
fooling myself, but my truth is always there, waiting to be released.

Death of my physical form works that way as well. All the
choices and all the events I experienced, lead up to that final day.
Funny thing is, it's not final at all. Just like the death and rebirth
of my cells while I'm alive, my consciousness still functions.
It is not controlled by time or space. I do stop focusing one part

of my consciousness on my physical form, and shift my focus to another reality. I am as alive as I was while experiencing the beliefs I had about death while living in this body. My after death experience could be completely different from yours, based on my thoughts about death. Interesting concept, but if I create my physical world by using my thoughts, I could also create my after life experience using my same consciousness. That idea brings a whole new concept to life. Fear can only be present if I think fearful thoughts.

In ignorance, I live in fear and create a world that doesn't exist either during this life or after. In love, I live connected to all life. In death, that connection grows, expands and becomes a grander version of this part of me. It consciously lives in harmony with another aspect of myself.

7. *Fuel for Thought*

I found a few thoughts I wanted to share today. Each paints a vision of who I am, or who I can be. There is always something special about reading something you already know. It's called remembering, bringing past knowledge into the present moment. It only takes a couple of minutes to change how I feel. Reading thoughts like these reminds me I'm not alone on my journey.

It is natural to experience contrast in life, so I can grow from it. The first thought is from Lao Tzu the "Ancient Boy" written over 2500 years ago:

Fame or integrity: Which is more important?
Money or happiness: Which is more valuable?
Success or failure: Which is more destructive?
If you look to others for fulfillment, you will never truly be fulfilled.
If your happiness depends on money, you will never be happy with yourself.
Be content with what you have, rejoice in the way things are.
When you realize there is nothing lacking, the whole world belongs to you.

The next thought is from Eva Pierrakos who was born in Vienna in 1915. She lectured across the world and her work became known as the Pathwork. She and her husband John, a psychiatrist, developed a school of therapy known as Core Energetics. This is one of Eva's works titled "Through the Gateway."
Through the gateway of feeling your weakness lies your strength.
Through the gateway of feeling your pain lies your pleasure and joy.
Through the gateway of feeling your fear lies your security and safety.
Through the gateway of feeling your loneliness lies your capacity to have fulfillment, love and companionship.

Through the gateway of feeling your hate lies your capacity to love.
Through the gateway of feeling your hopelessness lies your true
and justified hope.
Through accepting the lacks of your childhood lies your
fulfillment now.

The last two thoughts are from Barbara Ann Brennan, who
founded a school of self-healing and has written several books
on the art of healing yourself. These quotes are from her book,
Light Emerging.

It's not selfish to love yourself. Rather think of yourself as a cup
that can be filled. When your cup runs over, the love spills out to
those around us. You must love yourself in order to give love
to others.

The most epidemic health problem we have today is self-hatred.
The course of self-hatred is self-betrayal.

8. Hide And Seek Anyone?

We shall not cease from exploration and the end of all our exploring will be to arrive where we started and know the place for the first time.

T.S. Elliot wrote that in his poem "Little Gidding."

I travel through my physical life with a veil of forgetfulness covering my focused consciousness, but I can still find my way back home and reunite with my greater awareness, and think it's the first time. Now that's an interesting thought. I know a part of me, but I feel like there is more to me than I know. So, I start searching all over the place to find it only to discover it's hidden within me for the purpose of becoming a grander version of myself. That grander growth expands the web I am connected to, and the whole web expands, including the Source of the web. The next question is expand to where? Every step in this process of rediscovery reveals yet another road of forgetfulness. I have an eternity to remember, so no need to rush things, right?

On this amazing journey, I pick a special way to go. The path chosen has the freedom, awareness, connection and contrast I need to complete the journey. However, upon my arrival on this planet I forgot that I have them. I look outside myself to fulfill this lack of understanding. I find others who claim to have the truth and mystery solved. All I need to do is follow them to get where I want to go. No need to use my skills, it's much easier to follow, and not think about it. That's okay. It's my journey, and I can travel on it as long as I want. At some point, something will awaken my belief in myself. And, the world changes. It becomes my world, and I can create it by my thoughts. I can be what I came here to be—a creator who paints a canvas of beauty and love just like the one who created me.

I feel my way on my path with my emotions, and express myself in gratitude. I remember I am aware connected energy, which is the greatest gift I can give myself. I can share it with all life and reunite with another aspect of my consciousness.

There is no need to follow anyone or anything, but my feelings. I have all I need within me to live in peace, joy and love for that is what I create. That is what I give. That is what I am.

T.S. Elliot mentioned coming to the end of exploring, but I think he meant just one road in the process—death. I do know the place after death, for I have created it by my beliefs. It certainly is not the end, but it is the beginning to becoming what I seek.

9. I make Footprints!

Do not seek to follow in the footsteps of the men of old; seek what they sought.

Matsuo Kinsaku, better known as Basho, was born in Japan in 1644. He was a servant to Todo and they both shared the love of Haikai.

In this form of poetry a poet added verse set in 5-7-5 syllables as is Haiku and then another poet added 7-7 syllables. After Todo's sudden death in 1666, Basho continue to study and teach poetry and was recognized in Japan, for his simply and natural style. He is now known worldwide as one of the greatest Japanese poets ever.

As you can see from the quote above, Basho was a seeker. He studied the ancient writings and lives of great Japanese men, but did not try to duplicate their lives in his, he sought to understand them and grow from them. He developed a semi-Buddhist philosophy of greeting the mundane world rather than separating himself from it.

Basho's search is not much different than mine is today. The search is one of unity. How to unite my thoughts with those I share this physical journey with. I can read and study about the great thinkers that lived before me and try to put myself in their shoes, or I can accept and respect all of them and continue my quest for unity with my world of consciousness.

The ancient thinkers are connected to me in a collective consciousness that is part of who I am. I am an extension of thought that is continuing on the road to unity. In order to connect to those thoughts, I must first be united within myself. The consciousness that is focused on my physical journey must recognize that there are other consciousnesses that are a part of me as well each one in its own reality. Each one connected in Love.

That is not an easy thought to accept. I was never taught that in school, yet I always knew there was more to me than I expressed. The study of who I am is an individual journey but it is connected to a universal consciousness. The journey consists in remembering, not in discovery. In diversity we all remember differently. If it was done the same way, no one would grow and change. Diversity effects change.

So as Basho says, I need not try to be something or someone else in order to conform or fit into a certain life style. I have within me the consciousness of unity; I just need to remember it. In accepting diversity as the vehicle for change and growth, I can begin to remember. I can see all life as connected consciousness. I can understand the contrast that diversity brings and learn from it. I can begin to feel myself and express my emotions in love, not fear.

I see the footprints of others and remember. I make my own footprints and become what I have always been—a spirit having a human experience.

10. I'm a Little Square

The book, Flatland:A Romance of Many Dimensions, was written in 1884 by Edwin Abbott, and is still popular among mathematics and computer science students. The story is that Flatland was a two-dimensional world and seeing and knowing could only be seen and known in that plane; there was nothing above it or below it. Flatland was populated by a large number of Squares and Circles with a subculture of Triangles and an occasional Parallelogram. In the book, a Square tells how he awakened. It begins:

One sunny day in Flatland, a little Square saw a Circle coming toward him. He carried on with his usual activities, but it soon became obvious that this Circle was not like any he had seen before. This Circle kept getting larger and larger until it was clearly not just a Circle, but a Sphere. Square had heard about Spheres before, but he had always believed that they were just fairy tales or children's myths. This one, however, looked very real indeed. Frightened, Square began to run.

"Don't be afraid," called the Sphere, "I won't hurt you!"

The Square stopped and turned toward the stranger. Slowly backing away, he asked, "What are you, anyway?"

"I'm a Sphere."

"But, there are no Spheres in Flatland," Squared challenged.

"That may be so," gently replied the Sphere, "but Flatland is not all there is to life. There is more to life than the two dimensions with which you are familiar—much, much more, indeed. There is actually another dimension of which most of the citizens of Flatland are not aware at all. Spaceland is a wonderful world

with so much more freedom to see and move and play! But, you cannot enjoy it because all of you in Flatland have gotten used to looking only forward, back, and to the sides. Hardly anyone in Flatland ever looks up! If you did, you would see many wondrous forms far more exciting and fascinating than you have found in Flatland."

"How can I see these lovely sights?" young Square wondered aloud.

"Simply look up and you will see the whole picture," the Sphere explained. "In fact," Sphere went on, "you will be surprised to know that what you see in Flatland is actually a part of the third dimension. Those you see as Circles are actually Spheres, but because you see only in two dimensions, all you see is one plane of a much greater reality!"

"You will be happy to know that you and your friends are not just Squares, but you are actually facets of a marvelous and very practical form called a "Cube." The Triangles belong to a mystical design called "Pyramid," and that funny-looking family down the street that you laugh at, Mr. and Mrs. Ellipse, are actually components of a most important configuration called Egg. Alas, but you see none of these rich aspects of your life because you are so preoccupied with what is behind and in front of you. Oh, Square if you only knew how much, much more there is to life, you would dance with joy!" Sphere paused for a moment. She realized this was a lot for a little Square to absorb so quickly, and she wanted to give him time to awaken. "My dear Square, the universe is so much greater than you have imagined and now you are seeing things as they truly are, and indeed have always been. I am very happy for you."

The Square was astounded; yet somehow it made sense. Into his mind flashed some memories of having seen unusual shapes when he was just a few points old. He remembered seeing beautiful, dazzling configurations just before going to sleep or

*while traveling through the park of Diamonds. Then, he recalled
that when he had told his mother about them that she patted
him on one of his sides and told him he had a vivid imagination.
Eventually, he stopped seeing them. He didn't want to be
different from his friends.*

*The Sphere, shimmering before the young one, sensed he was ready
to see more. "Would you like to see your true self?" she asked.*

*The Square hesitated. He wasn't quite sure about his true self.
It seemed that most of the inhabitants of Flatland were rather
fearful of looking at their true self. Whenever someone would
bring up the idea of their true self at a party, for example, someone
would quickly make a joke or change the subject. Why were the
Flatlanders so afraid of their own being? Even the Square could
not understand why hardly anyone in Flatland loved himself.*

*"Yes," Square answered, "Yes I would like to see my true self."
The moment he said those words, his fear went away.*

*"Very well, then. Look up!" Sphere commanded. "Look up and
you will see who you really are!"*

*Square looked up and he could hardly believe his eyes. What a
wondrous sight he did see! He saw that he was not just a small
Polygon with four sides of equal length, as he had read in his
Geometric Genealogy textbook. He saw that his square self was
just one part of his being, the part that could be seen in Flatland.
Square saw that he was actually a great, glowing Cube of which
the lines that he thought limited him were but one aspect.
How exciting to find that he was a whole! So that was why he
had felt so strangely incomplete as a little Square! Now he
realized that there was nothing to be afraid of. Nothing in his
real self could harm him. In fact, nothing had ever made him as
happy as looking upon his real self and seeing all that he was.*

That was just the beginning. As the Square became more and more comfortable looking up, he could see the real identity of everyone in Flatland! They were so beautiful! He saw marvelous Cones, sparkling Cylinders, and even a Great Sphere made up of triangles. His guide told him this was a "Geodesic Dome" (but hardly anyone in Flatland was ready for that one). Square saw that what was happening in Flatland was such a little part of the whole picture. And he was afraid no more.

I live in a three dimensional world and I am scared to see and feel the other dimensions that surround me. By looking within I am able to see my true self; I am able to feel whole, and just like the Square, I'm not afraid anymore.

11. Unformed or Cooked?

Unformed people delight in the gaudy and in novelty.
Cooked people delight in the ordinary.

That's an old Zen saying and as you know, it can mean whatever you think it does. My life has been filled with novelty and gaudiness at times and as I think about it, I was a bit "unformed" in my thinking. I showered myself with all sorts of material things to act ordinary; ordinary I thought was what everyone else was doing in the quest for riches. My self-esteem was based on what I possessed, not how I felt. The world and life was a place to get as much as I could in order to be extra-ordinary. That was the mark of excellence, being above ordinary. I wanted to be at the top of ordinary in every way, but found myself in a state of confusion, frustration, and emptiness. The more I got, the more I wanted, and this cycle became my life. I was living to get, not living to just be in the moment and feel the beauty of physical existence. I was extremely "unformed," but didn't see myself that way. I was part of the herd, fighting to be on top of this pile of ordinariness.

Something happened to me. I was cooked by events in my life. Several situations developed and I changed my thinking. These situations presented themselves to me at different times, but each one cooked me in a special way until I was completely baked. The real meaning of ordinary appeared before me and I fell off the plate of wanting and onto the table of living.

I began to feel myself in every moment. I sensed my emotions in another form, and they became my guidance system for learning. My life was no longer a measuring stick of useless "things," each moment brought the gift of awareness into focus. The "things" were external and ordinary was internal.

People and places became special treats. All of them gave me something I could use to be ordinary—a smile, a joke, the view of a sunset or the feel of a cool stream. They all made me feel grateful. Friends and family filled me with a sense of wellness and their words and actions reinforced my thoughts. Ordinary was more than I expected it to be; it was living my truth, and sharing myself in unconditional service.

Now, I am ordinary in a non-ordinary way; I'm cooked and formed into another version of myself. I get excited when I open my eyes and feel a new day. I live each moment and learn and grow from the experiences of physical life. I ask for help and receive it from my source, and ordinary becomes my state of being—the essence of my expression.

12. Where Are My Keys?

Act without doing; work without effort. Think of the small as large and the few as many. Confront the difficult while it is still easy; accomplish the great task by a series of small acts. The Master never reaches for the great; thus she achieves greatness. When she runs into difficulty, she stops and gives herself to it. She doesn't cling to her own comfort; thus problems are not problems for her.

Lao-tzu, the Chinese recluse, wrote those words over 2500 years ago.

It's interesting that I somehow thought that ancient people were so far behind our modern day thoughts. Now, I realize it's the other way around. The more I remember, the more I understand that we have left the door to knowing locked by distorted truths and beliefs. Our minds have been placed in a box of fear, and the lid is covered with misconceptions.

Lao-tzu's words ring out like a stadium filled with high school cheerleaders. I make the simple things in life difficult. I act by doing, pushing, and forcing. I work in stress, anger, and judgment. I try to cut corners in order to achieve a great task. I reach for greatness when I don't feel great. I think of the few as not enough, and the many as nowhere near enough. I confront the difficult by running away from it. I look at myself and see disappointment, loneliness, and depression. The door to knowing is locked and I have lost the keys.

Lao-tzu uses the word "master" to signify oneness within us. All the acts he describes are thoughts I live daily. It is how I think that creates the problems or lack of problems. I have the keys to unlock the door of knowing. I just need to reach inside of me and use them.

I have feelings and emotions that will show me the way to act if I allow them the freedom to work. I have ancient wisdom within me that will teach me if I allow it to speak. I have unlimited love surrounding me; all I need to do is to let it in by my positive thoughts. I have a center of Divine Oneness that is waiting for me to remember it by accepting and touching it with my thoughts. These keys unlock my door and I begin to live in harmony.

No major surgeries or dramas to deal with; just an awakening within myself that changes my beliefs. I begin to experience those beliefs and then express them. I become the symbol of peace, the symbol for abundance, the symbol for love.

Quite a key chain, don't you think?

13. Which Road Is It?

I had a conversation with a friend this week and he was very concerned with the state of things in America, as well as the world. He correctly identified all the problems that were having an impact on his thoughts. He was upset with the follies of different governments, business, politics, schools, and society in general. He was convinced there was no solution to the problems, and believed that we all were facing destruction in some manner. It seemed that expressing his views to me relieved his concern for the moment. He asked me what I thought about all the information he shared with me, and I told him I lived in a different world. That of course did not make much sense to him. He knew all he described to me was very real and I was also part of all the gloom he presented. Was I ignoring reality? Was I ignorant of world events? Or was I just plain stupid?

I told my friend that my thoughts create my world and I saw a different world evolving. Not one of despair and destruction, but one of unity, abundance and peace. I told him it started with me. I would live in a world that, in spite of all the daily contrast, would become a grander version of itself, a place of love, because that is what I believed. It all starts with my thoughts.

I found the words of Confucius where I had written them in one of my books in 2003. Confucius did not begin a religion, he was known as a moral reformer. He was born in 551 B.C. He died 70 years later in 479 B.C. He believed and learned from his ancients that the road to change starts with the individual. He explains that in this work written over 2,000 years ago.

The illustrious ancients, when they wished to make clear and to propagate the highest virtues in the world, put their states in proper order. Before putting their states in order, they regulated their families. Before regulating their families they cultivated

their own selves, they perfected their souls. Before perfecting
their souls they tried to be sincere in their thoughts. Before they
tried to be sincere in their thoughts, they extended to the utmost
their knowledge. Such investigation of knowledge lay in the
investigation of things, and in seeing them as they really were.
When things were thus investigated, knowledge becomes complete.
When knowledge was complete, their thoughts became sincere.
When their thoughts were sincere, their souls became perfect.
When their souls were perfect, their own selves became cultivated.
When their selves were cultivated, their families became regulated.
When their families were regulated, their states came to be put
in proper order. When their states were in proper order, then
the whole world became peaceful and happy.

Sounds like a new, old way of thinking. Or, should I say
remembering?

Breakthrough

1. You're Welcome!

Giving thanks is a global tradition. Every culture offers gratitude to someone or something for the state of their reality at any given moment in time.

Thanks are the prayers of life; they are the hymns of acceptance and the oracles of peace. Thanks have no racial, political or religious agenda; they are flowing gestures of free will. The earth, its animals, plants and humans, all have their own way of expressing gratitude; each life form lives to be in a state of grateful existence. The abundance that manifests from this gratitude is unending and unstoppable, even if I choose to ignore it through thoughts of lack.

William Stanley Merwin born in 1927 is one of the most influential poets of the 20th century. He wrote about saying "Thank you," in the human way. The condition called being "human," is a mixed event, filled with contrast and chaos. Each human life has its own set of values and standards that brings a sense of normalcy to the framework of survival. Each person gives thanks for their situation even when it is hard to find anything to be thankful for. Merwin explains the condition some of us find ourselves living in, and he brings the thought of thanks into that arena of darkness. From these thoughts of thanks, the light appears and this awareness brings connection to a separated species longing for unity.

Listen
With the night falling we are saying thank you
We are stopping on the bridge to bow from the railings
We are running out of the glass rooms
With our mouths full of food to look at the sky
And say thank you
We are standing by the water looking out

In different directions
Back from a series of hospitals back from a mugging
After funerals we are saying thank you
After the news of the dead
Whether or not we knew them we are saying thank you
Looking up from tables we are saying thank you
In a culture up to its chin in shame
Living in the stench it has chosen we are saying thank you

Over telephones we are saying thank you
In doorways and in the back of cars and in elevators
Remembering wars and the police at the back door
And the beatings on stairs we are saying thank you
With the crooks in office with the rich and fashionable
Unchanged we go on saying thank you thank you

With the animals dying around us
Our lost feelings we are saying thank you
With the forests falling faster than the minutes
Of our lives we are saying thank you
With the words going out like cells of a brain
With the cities growing over us like the earth
We are saying thank you faster and faster
With nobody listening we are saying thank you
We are saying thank you and waving
Dark though it is

Waving, I find time to say thank you. Physical life is now, and
new thoughts manifest within my mind. Change brings new
energy to my human consciousness and my gestures of thanks,
become louder and more frequent. With this change my life
is measured not by my mistakes, but by my truth. I accept the
contrast and chaos and say thank you, knowing I am becoming
a grander version of who I am. Positive energy surrounds me
and I cherish all life forms and forgive myself for the temporary
insanity of being human. I can hear the sound of nature saying
thank you and I say, "You're welcome."

161

2. A Struggle-free Reality

When you find yourself struggling to manipulate and control external events in your life, look at the fear which lies beneath these actions. If you would simply give up and allow the flow of events, stating your preferred outcome, you would find that the results will be exactly as you desired without the struggle.

Jani King, the Australian Ph.D, wrote those words in her book The Gift. When I read her words the first time I realized that giving up, and allowing are not the kind of things I have been taught to do. Fighting and controlling any situation are the methods I used to achieve what I wanted. I had been taught that if I didn't assert my emotions into the event, then I wasn't really trying to be successful. Instead, I was being lazy, stupid, and non-conforming—words that put me in a state of fear. I wanted to please others. I had to be strong and stubborn to get what I wanted and thought I needed, at any cost. The more I struggled to reach things, the farther away they seemed to get and the more frustrated I became.

Jani's words are simple, in fact, too simple to be true in this world of super powers where the person with the most gets more and those with the least get even less. The twentieth century honored power, wars, and merciless acts of vengeance as a means to be the victor and the leader with an illusion of greatness. Those thoughts filtered down through each individual and it was the way life had to be lived in order to get what I needed to be successful. All of it was senseless acts of ego trying to protect the fear that supports this misguided feeling of self-righteousness.

Jani also said, "Enlightenment is not about being good. It is about BEING."

It's about allowing the energy of the universe to flow through me. It's about giving that energy to others. When I release myself to this power, I no longer need to push and pull to get results; I see them already manifested. They will come into my experience when my vibration is in sync with my desire. All the fear and anger I use to try to force results, only holds my desire at a different vibration and I am frustrated into thinking that the world is an evil, hateful place. I create the situation by making a choice to struggle rather than to allow. When I embrace my ego and begin to forgive myself and give up the need to control, my experiences change. The universe hears my request not with words, but with feelings. Feelings and emotions are the language of the universe. They measure my vibration and if I am open and my will is clear, my request is fulfilled almost immediately.

The awareness of enlightenment, the natural way of being, is acceptance—acceptance of my own ego, as well as my inner self that is connected to ALL THERE IS. I don't need instructions or a course in philosophy to achieve this state of knowing; all I need is my will to do it. Once I drop all the tools I use to hide my fears, and embrace myself in love, my desires begin to materialize. I live in a state where there are no limitations. As long as I follow my truth, the universe gives me abundance, peace and the power of forgiveness. I am dressed in gratitude and the world becomes a struggle-free reality.

3. *Comparisons are Odious*

Comparisons are odious.

These words were popular in the fourteenth century. It's amazing that seven centuries later comparisons are the measurement of success, not disgust. How did the thought of disgust become the norm in my world?

I compare and am compared in almost everything. The mark of success in business is beating last year's accomplishment. The feeling of pride has to do with measuring the square feet in my home and comparing it to that of my friend's home. The length of my formal education is compared to others in order to secure a job. Where I stand on religion, politics and justice is how I am accepted and compared in society. It seems no matter what endeavor I choose, I am compared with someone or something in order to define who I am.

If I do not meet the standards of the comparison, I feel rejected or defeated and I sink into a mild form of depression. Then, I think I am not worthy to be me because I'm told I'm not good enough. I begin to believe those thoughts, and live my life through the thoughts of others. I compare myself to others who have those same feelings, and a whole group of us function in a world of "not good enough." I find myself locked in negativity and all I see and attract are those thoughts.

Maybe my peers in the fourteenth century had it right. What is the point of comparing? What do I gain by feeling superior to others? What power do I gain by believing I am better than everyone else? Comparison creates separation. Does it achieve the mark of excellence that I search for in order to be a noble human? Is there such thing as good and bad, right and wrong in the eyes of my creator? Does this lifestyle bring me happiness and the feeling of well-being I seek daily, or is it an illusion created by me to fill the void of not really knowing who I am?

I have the ability to be who I am without comparison. I can reach inside myself and find the leader I seek. I can discover the friend who accepts everyone's path. I can be the worker who gives service to others without conditions. I can be the student who passes all exams with the highest grade—an inner feeling of self-esteem. I need not look for the approval of others if I follow my emotions and am connected to my source of energy. I have already compared myself to my creator and I am his expression. That awareness is the comparison of the twenty-first century.

To live in unity in spite of diversity is the mark of excellence. To accept my physical journey as a lesson in growth and expansion is the sign of freedom. Freedom is love. Love does not compare, it becomes ALL THERE IS.

4. Enlighten What?

If being right is your goal, you will find error in the world, and seek to correct it. But do not expect peace of mind. If peace of mind is your goal, look for the errors in your beliefs and expectations. Seek to change them, not the world.

Many sages have written this quote over the years, in many languages. Each one understands that the ultimate feeling of peace is within all of us, not waiting for us to discover it externally. The now-age term "enlightenment" has a cloudy definition attached to it. Many believe it pertains to a new religion, a new form of salvation, or a fix for what ails us internally. We have called many people enlightened ones. We have worshipped them for years in our churches and religious services. It seems they were more than human or that they were more than we are. But, if you study the physical lives of these people, you discover they lived the same way we do, had the same life dramas and felt the same emotions as we experience. But something in their lives changed and they became something other than human—something worth worshipping. What is this change that makes the ordinary, extraordinary?

The quote above reminds me how to become enlightened. It starts with me and ends with me. I have the ability to look within and discover a part of me that has been hidden by my belief system. If I open myself and allow my feelings and emotions to guide me, I start to see another me. I begin to feel there is more to me than mind and body. I see a connected web of life in a connected universe. New thoughts bring back old memories. I light a part of me that has been in the dark. I turn my consciousness and see more consciousness in an endless world of joy.

They are some of us that do not want this new way of thinking. They say that the old one works just fine. If it has gotten me this far, no need to change now, right? Right, your beliefs are yours. Your life is your journey and it is what you want it to be. Whatever the belief, it will take you where you want to go. You have the choice to experience whatever makes you happy in any form you choose. In your own way, you are enlightened. You are living your beliefs and creating the world you live in. If you are happy in that world, you have been enlightened. You are experiencing what you create. Enlightenment is the understanding that you create your own experience by what you believe. You have made a choice and you become it.

Part of the now-age information that is becoming available is misunderstood. I can live my life in any way I choose to believe. I may not feel uncomfortable with new ideas. Diversity makes the now-age possible, because if not for change, we would stagnant in our own pool of sameness. I believe we are all enlightened in one way or another. My path is different from my parents and friends, and that's okay. We are all here to learn and we all pass the test. No grade is necessary to graduate. How I treat others is how I think about myself, and that is the lesson I am here to learn. The good news is, I can repeat the lesson as many times as I want.

5. *My Trash is Less Trashy!*

As with language, so with life: Less is often more. The quality of life is marked by what you can do without and still do well. The best things in life aren't. Simplify. Thoreau subscribed to this line of thinking. So did Buddha, Lao-tzu and Jesus. Possession is nine-tenths of our flaw.

Robert Fulghum was born in 1937 and wrote the book, "All I Really Need to Know I learned in Kindergarten." He is a Unitarian minister, artist and teacher and lives in the state of Washington.

He says a lot in the short quote above. Less is more when you think that way. I realized how much stuff I had by the amount of trash I accumulated over a week. The more trash I had, the more I wanted to buy. I was living in the economic powerhouse of spending money, time, and people in the quest to be wealthy and to be recognized.

It is a game of catching shadows; there is always a bigger one to catch. These shadows kept getting bigger and they were ever present to badger me with visions of grandeur. Caught in this game, my life became confused, cluttered and stress filled. Nothing was satisfying, no matter what the cost. Trash had become my badge of identity.

As Fulgrum tells me, that thinking is self-defeating. I found what I had been searching for without spending a penny. I found my ability to remember who I am, and my world changed. I no longer measured myself by material gains or losses. I have no need for expensive jewelry or clothing. I no longer need to support the new car industry, my "new," old one works as well. I find abundance everywhere I look. I feel the power of self-assurance in purchase less freedom.

In remembering, I find my freedom and my free will. I can share and give and experience abundance. If my thoughts focus on a desire, it manifests, if I think about negativity that is what I express. I began to change my thoughts and my world became a positive experience. By thinking about love and knowing I am an expression of love I can satisfy all my desires and be happy.

The external shadows are disappearing in forgiveness and self-love. My ego is still present, but is now operating through my innate feelings and emotions. My spirit guides me and I follow with joy.

My trash is less trashy and more rewarding. It is now a symbol of freedom, not of power.

6. Here's To Self-Being

The mind as it is in itself, is free of ills; this is the precept of self being. The mind as it is in itself is free from disturbances; this is the meditation of self-being. The mind as it is in itself is free from follies; this is the knowledge of self being.

Hui-neng was born in 638 AD in Canton. He is the sixth patriarch of Chinese Chan Buddhism. He is considered the founder of Sudden Enlightenment, a Southern Chan school of Buddhism.

It seems that Hui-neng had the correct idea; we are free from illness, disturbances and folly, if we think we are. That's exactly what quantum physics is telling us. So the idea is not new. It is simply misunderstood through distorted beliefs.

My beliefs create the world I live in. I don't need someone else's beliefs to rule my life. I just need to be aware of the creativity I have within me. Once I release myself from the jail of someone else's thoughts, I can start to feel myself, and let my innate guidance system show me the abundance that surrounds me. My thoughts attract what I see around me. If I see illness, disturbances and folly, then that's my world. I can also attract peace, abundance and love, and my world becomes those things. Simply by changing what I think, I begin to move the collective consciousness in that direction.

Someone said that if just over one percent of the world's population thought about their true state of being, the change we want to see in the world would be manifested and would begin immediately. It's like that 100-monkey theory a study group of scientist performed on a family of primates on an island. The primates had learned a behavior from another family on the same island. However, the two families had never had contact with each other. They began to do the same task because their instincts were connected to the collective consciousness of their species. That is the knowledge of self-being and it works with humans too.

My truth tells me that my self-being is free. Free to experience all the things I desire on my physical journey. Allowing them to become my world is my choice. I become what I think, and I think the world is beginning to awaken from a long sleep.

Here's to self-being, our true nature and the nature of all life.

7. Here's to the End

*The world as we know it is coming to an end. The world as
the center of the universe, the world divided from the heavens,
the world bound by horizons in which love is reserved for the
members of the in group: that is the world that is passing away.
The Apocalypse does not point to a fiery Armageddon but to the
fact that our ignorance and our complacency are coming to an end.*

Joseph Campbell was born in White Plains, New York in 1904.
His life was dedicated to learning and teaching. He was a
professor at Sarah Lawrence College for 38 years. He studied
Native American history, medieval literature earning a M.A. in
1927, and went on to become an expert in mythology.

George Lucas used Campbell's work as a resource while Star
Wars was being produced. Lucas wrote several books, and was
interviewed by Bill Moyers on a PBS special. He certainly
understood how we are moving through time, based on what he
had studied about the past.

Joseph said the world, as we know it, is coming to an end.
I certainly can relate to that. I think we all can. If nothing
else, computers are reshaping our worldwide view, and if they
continue developing at the current rate, by 2020 a personal
computer will have more power and speed than all the
computers in Silicon Valley in 1998. And that is just the tip of
the change.

The information revolution is outpacing the industrial and
agricultural revolutions, which means that human
evolution is moving even faster. But moving where? Space or
sea exploration? Perhaps, but my inner revolution represents the
direction of ephemeral thinking, the trend toward doing more
with less. It takes less matter and energy to modify computer

software than it does the engine of automobiles, but it takes even less to change my mind. All signs are pointing to the new discovery—the world within myself. My attitudes, mental habits, and assumptions as to who I am and what I can achieve are my new world. The change I experience happens faster than I realize once I understand that my thoughts create the world I live in.

Living in my world does leave the old one behind just like realizing the physical world is round instead of flat. As Campbell said my ignorance and complacency are coming to an end, just by changing my thoughts. No fires or destruction; only new thoughts about connection and awareness—new visions of life and the excitement of creation. A new attitude brings unity and love for all life into my world. It only takes a thought to make it so. I am what I think, and my thoughts make my world.

8. Infinite Play Anyone?

The big game, the big race, the big competition; who is going to win?
We all want to, right? How many lives are built around the power
of winning? The feeling of winning has changed the lives of
so many. Of course, defeat has done the same thing. One thing
is for sure; the winner and the loser will change in some way.
What the change is depends on the kind of game I play.

Win or lose the ultimate prize in all the games I play is the
change I feel within myself. Life itself is a game, and I change
every second. My cells and organs are always changing and
modifying the body I exist in. My mind is capturing and
intercepting thoughts from my consciousness that change
my world. My spirit is guiding me in all my perceptions and
the probabilities that are created; in one big game of change.
So what is the nature of these games? How can I describe how
I feel about them? I found something that might answer those
questions from James P. Carse, who was a professor of history
and the literature of religion at NYU. It is from his 1986 book
"Finite and Infinite Games."

"There are at least two kinds of games. One could be called
finite, the other infinite.
A finite game is played for the purpose of winning, an infinite
game for the purpose of continuing to play.
Finite players play within boundaries; infinite players play
with boundaries.
Surprise causes finite play to end; it is the reason for infinite
play to continue.
To be prepared against surprise is to be trained. To be
prepared for surprise is to be educated.
The finite play for life is serious; the infinite play of life is joyous.
The joyfulness of infinite play, its laughter, lies in learning to
start something we cannot finish.
No one can play a game alone. One cannot be human by oneself.

Our social existence has ... an inescapably fluid character.
... We are not the stones over which the stream of the world
flows; we are the stream itself.
Change itself is the very basis of our continuity as persons.
Only that which can change can continue; this is the principle
by which infinite players live."

We are all infinite players. Sometimes we act as finite players,
but then we change.
It is through these changes that I experience and express who
I am. I grow into a grander version of myself. As Carse says, our
purpose is to continue to play in joyfulness, laughter and learning.
That game has no losers.

9. The Sheltered Life!

"I am a writer who came from a sheltered life. A sheltered life can
be a daring life as well. For all serious daring starts from within."

Eudora Alice Welty was born in 1909. She was a photographer,
Pulitzer Prize winning writer, and a gracious lady from Jackson
Mississippi. She dedicated most of her life to writing fiction and
her works immediately established her as a leading figure in
American Literature especially the American South.

Her words above bring a sense of unity to life; we all live a
sheltered life to begin with, for we all start our journey from within.
I overlooked that concept for many years, the external world had a
grip on me and I fell into the trap of materialism. I was hooked
on the right and wrong approach to every situation and there
was someone or something that was always causing me pain
and aggravation. I captured the daring life by wrestling with
judgment and fear, the self-created feelings that arise from being
separated from my inner world. I did live a sheltered life because
I only lived in one reality, which held me captive because I was
too weak to listen to my inner voice. I followed the crowd in
order to conform and found myself in a cell of insanity looking
for help and wanting permission to live.

Well, that's all behind me. I understand who I am. I appreciate the world I have within myself and explore it everyday. It is a journey of consciousness that brings me to many crossroads and choices. It is a world of probabilities and possibilities where things form into matter and manifest into things. I am a co-creator of my life and each moment is an experience worth living. From my choices I learn lessons and grow from the changes that the lesson teach me. I expand my sheltered existence into a world of color and beauty where there is consciousness in everything. I continue to expand and feel the excitement that living my truth brings me through the interaction I have with all living things. The shelter of unity changes my thoughts and I see without judgment, fear or anger. Each experience is an expression of daring where I guide myself with gratitude and appreciation.

Eudora understood all of that. She wrote about it and lived it. The time to start living is a personal choice. We all do it at different times and in different lives. Some only do it in dreams and others do it all the time. In our diversity we become one, because from that contrast we learn to become grander versions of ourselves; the version that starts from within, the spirit that is having a human experience in order to remember. Remembering is awakening. Awakening is connection. The connection of my spirit to All There is in a web of love that continues to expand and grow as I do.

The sheltered life is the life we all want to experience, for it is real. It is real because I know who I am. In that knowing, I am connected to the shelter of unity, which opens, and I begin to feel the presence of another reality and the concept of eternal life. From within comes answers; from within comes questions; from within comes the consciousness to live both.

10. Outrageous? It Doesn't Matter!

"Recognize what does not matter, and if your brother asks you for something "outrageous" do it because it does not matter. Refuse and your opinion establishes that it does matter to you. It is only you, therefore, who have made the request outrageous..."

That's from the "Course In Miracles," a wonderful book of thoughts. It's about forgiveness. Forgiving yourself first and then being able to forgive anyone you may come in contact with and experienced some kind of pain. If I am in that place of peace within myself, I change my world. The Course also says, *"It is not up to you to change your brother, but merely to accept him as he is."* Now that is well worth remembering, I can't tell you how many times I have wanted to change someone into something other than themselves. Instead of focusing my attention on what I could change, I threw myself into someone Else's business.

Someone once said: *"There are two types of business: yours and the other person's. Many people can't tell them apart."*

So true, no doubt I think it easier to try to change others instead of my self. Where do I begin to change, and do I want to? I'm doing OK as I am, right?

I have different answers and ask that question at different times, but I will change. Not because someone told me to, but because I want to. At some point something touches me that brings me closer to who I am, and it comes in many forms. The list is long, religion of all kinds is life changing, whether it is Eastern or Western thought. Meditation, yoga, dreaming, daily events, success, failure, and my friends, create an environment for change. What I believe will be the change. It will be what I experience, express and become.

That brings me back to what the Course says; *"It doesn't matter, unless you make it so."*

I make my world what it is by my beliefs, and no one can change them unless I want them to. I can be forgiving, sharing, compassionate and happy or not, after all, it is I who grabs a thought each morning and creates a part of my life.

My belief now is: ask me to do something "outrageous," and I'll do it, because to me, it doesn't matter.

I set the mood for my thoughts and I attract what I think about; which is forgiveness, gratitude and Love.

In the world of outrageous-ness, that's all that matters.

11. I Dare to Be Myself!

"We have to dare to be ourselves, however frightening or strange that self may prove to be."

Mary Sarton born in 1912 is an American writer and poet. She wrote over 53 books: 19 novels and 17 books of poetry, 15 nonfiction works including her acclaimed journals, 2 children's books a play and some screenplays. The Sarton Fund was established after her death to provide scholarships for poets and historians of science. (Her father was a historian of science at Harvard)

Dare to be ourselves is an interesting thought. I travel on my journey through time wondering who I am. Trying to discover the real me through various methods and experiences, I see a part of myself, but it seems like I am not completely awake; some inner voice keeps calling me and I think it has the wrong number. I know what I have been taught; my religious training and other courses in life tell me there is more to me than I can understand; so I live the human part of me conforming to the labels that society has given me. I am a prefabricated version of myself thanks to the physical world that I believe in.

Mary also said: *"I think of the trees and how simply they let go, let fall the riches of a season, how without grief (it seems) they can let go and go deep into their roots for renewal and sleep."*

What if I begin to act like the trees, instead of hanging on to everything I consider riches, power and glory? What if I shed my leaves of fear and put my faith in the hands of the universe, and feel the cycle of my seasons? What if I go within myself, to the roots that support my physical body and ask for help from my greater consciousness? Perhaps then I can begin to know who I am and what my intentions are. Perhaps then I can call myself whole and not fear the unknown darkness of death. My truth is worth the pain of discovery and it is the holy grail of life.

Mary said a lot of things that are all worth reading and appreciating. Two of them are: *"Each day, and the living of it, has to be a conscious creation in which discipline and order are relieved with some play and pure foolishness."*

"True feeling justifies whatever it may cost".

She's got a point, I do want to play and be foolish and these acts make me feel good. When I feel good my vibrations attract more good. I then experience a sense of well being that lifts my thoughts and directs me on my journey. Finding another aspect of who I am is worth the cost; it is worth the effort to be united in consciousness. I am the only one that can do that for myself and I deserve to experience and express myself completely in physical form. I have a reservoir of love within me, and it is waiting for the dam of separation to crack, so I can water my tree of life with the unity of All There Is, Love.

My complete self is not scary; it's not strange. It is who I am. Just like the trees I can find comfort in my roots and renew my journey. I can grow and change and know that I am experiencing the meaning of life and share myself in gratitude and service and have a lot of fun.

12. New Ideas? Or Forgotten Ones?

I have two thoughts from distant friends that I want to share with you. The first is from Rainer Maria Rilke, a twentieth century visionary who wrote in German:

I know that nothing has ever been real,
without my beholding it.
All becoming has needed me.
My looking ripens things and they come toward me,
To meet and be met.

The second one is from the Dalai Lama when the Chinese asked him about the invasion of his country:

Why didn't you fight back against the Chinese? The Dalai Lama
looked down, swung his feet, then looked back up and said, Well
war is obsolete, you know. Of course the mind can rationalize
fighting back, but the heart, the heart would never understand.
Then you would be divided in yourself, the heart and the mind,
and the war would be inside you.

I think Rilke's thought from the book Love Poems to God explains in different words what the Dalai Lama said. Both thoughts create new ideas for me to explore.

13. *Nothing Happened and I Want to Report It!*

Perhaps all the dragons of our lives are princesses who are only waiting to see us once, beautiful and brave. Perhaps everything "Terrible" is in its deepest being something that needs our love...

The great poet Rainer Maria Rilke understood the power of Love way back at the turn of the twentieth century. There is nothing else, but love.
I believe in synchronicity and that the things I experience day by day teach me about love. Even the news, where it's hard to find love, teaches me it's there, if I see it. Lessons and wisdom catch me by surprise sometimes.

I just read this morning that there is a newspaper called *The Dot* that has the motto: "Nothing Happened and We Want to Report It." It is a wonderful non- dualistic thought that there is nothing but love in the world. It doesn't happen; it is, and there is plenty of news in that story.

A friend of mine posted a great story about love on her blog. The story was written by Joe Vitale, author and motivational speaker. He injects all his thoughts about everything with the word love. Whether it is the normal acts he accomplishes daily or the books he writes, he blesses everything with his thoughts of love. He is experiencing amazing results. One example he notes is that his latest book became a bestseller before it was even published. Visit: **http://kathleenjacoby.blogs.com/** to read Kathleen's article about Joe.

Rilke tells us that the violence, hatred, anger, and the fear we face have love in them if we project our love into them. I breathe out love and compassion, and breathe in hatred, anger and judgment for the simple purpose of accepting the things as they are. Then, I add forgiveness and release them by exhaling. By doing so, I am changing my perception of them. Each act and event of every day can be felt that way for my feelings are my prayers of love. I change my reality by feeling. No one else can do it for me.

With a change of perception, my life changes. I am no longer a victim. I see myself as complete because I am one with ALL THERE IS, love. My life is filled with meaning, with abundance. Whatever I desire is manifested. I control my life with thoughts of unity. I become who I am, and want to expand within that knowledge. Physically and mentally I ignite my spirit. My spirit has been waiting for me to feel the power of love that is the essence of life. I love this opportunity to share these words with you. I love you for reading them, and I love reporting, "Nothing is happening."

14. What Will it Take To Change?

Will transformation be inspired with flame, where something eludes you, resplendent with change?

Ranier Maria Rilke was a turn of the twentieth century European poet. His work has inspired me for several years.

As you can see from his words, he certainly understood the need for change. With the elections coming up, it seems the media is hot on the trail of a new leader. I watched a young, articulate, well-educated candidate on the news the other night and he seemed to be honest, caring, intelligent, and perhaps a good choice to lead our country. Of course, at least 80% of us at election time feel that their candidate has these same qualities, and yet when they are elected, we find ourselves still wanting change.

The candidates themselves want change, but once in the position to make that change, other agendas surface, and we find confusion, distrust, and disappointment to be our change.

As Rilke said, be inspired by flame, the flame is my truth that burns within me. Not a distorted truth that is based on control. Commandments based on fear, judgment, and sin seem to be a truth that has not supplied a change. But if I change the word commandment to commitment, it's something I want to do, not out of fear of retribution, but out of love.

Here is my version of the Ten Commandants, as Ten Commitments:

1. I commit to Freedom. I am free to create my life in joy, enfolded in love. I give and share the pure expression of who I am.

2. I commit to authenticity, knowing that I'm connected to

Source Love and that is who I am—never doubting that I create my world of truth, physically and spiritually.

3. I commit to acceptance, remembering who I am, and why I am traveling my physical path. I know all paths lead to the same love, and that I desire to expand within that love, as does all life.

4. I commit to relax, knowing all is well. My love of self brings me to a place of peace that guides me when my thoughts rest.

5. I commit to wholeness by being connected to all those around me, eternally in love; appreciating the thoughts of kindness given to me by all my angels, I feel an everlasting gratitude for life.

6. I commit to forgiveness. First I forgive myself, and then in remembering forgiveness, all I perceive will be all I become in a mirror of love.

7. I commit to love—to the union of two souls in truth, understanding that love is free, without anger, fear, judgment, or shame. It is the pure union of spirit manifested physically.

8. I commit to abundance by realizing I have all I need within myself to create a life of no needs. ALL THERE IS is waiting for me abundantly.

9. I commit to truth. I am and will be true to myself first. Then all I see is truth, from my Source.

10. I commit to peace. My truth is knowing that my life is peace, which creates wings of desire that fly with eyes of oneness.

With these commitments, I can be the change I want to see. I will experience and express and become the changes and my world begins to change.

15. Which Way is the Door?

The world of the mind encloses the whole universe in its light.
It is a cosmic life and a cosmic spirit, and at the same time an
individual life and an individual spirit.

D.T. Suzuki was a turn of the twentieth century teacher of
Zen Buddhism in Japan. He is credited with being a pioneer
in teaching Zen outside of Japan and his writings are vast and
enlightening. I don't have to practice the religion of Buddhism to
understand what he was teaching in the above quote. The world
of the mind is my reality and I am connected to the universe in
consciousness.

Plato, the Greek philosopher born around 428 B.C., wrote about
reality and how much of it we are really aware of. Somewhere in
our history, we closed our minds to certain beliefs and created a
world that is an illusion.

Plato maintained that man, in his natural state, is living like he
is sitting in a cave, with his back facing the opening of the cave.
Outside this opening lies the light of eternal reality. But man,
because his back is to the light, sees only the shadows of reality
dancing across the back of the cave, and with his attention on
the wall, sees only dreams and reflections, never reality itself.
So fascinated is man with these shadows that he builds great
systems of science and philosophy around these phantoms.
Then one day, somebody escapes from the cave and sees reality.
He returns to the cave and says, "Guys you're not going to
believe this but..."

There are many people escaping from that cave today to see their
own reality. There is so much information available to assist
anyone who feels the need to escape. Feeling is the language of
our complete self, the one that D.T. Suzuki talks about. We have
the ability to walk out of the cave at anytime, and feel the
grander self that rests within us.

We are all connected, but we are individuals who create the world we live in. Each of us does it differently and that is the wonder of contrast. It allows us to experience and expand our own world and become the cosmic spirit that expresses love for all life. Separation becomes obsolete, and unity reigns supreme. Compassion, gratitude, and sharing are universal. Love of self is the vessel that holds love for our reality. Prayer is the feeling of achievement. Achievement is the joy of connection. Connection is the universal experience of love. Love is ALL THERE IS.

Flow

1. A Cling-less Creature

Once there lived a village of creatures along the bottom of a great crystal river. Each creature in its own manner clung tightly to the twigs and rocks of the river bottom; for clinging was their way of life, and resisting the current was what each had learned from birth. But one creature said at last, "I am tired of clinging. Though I cannot see it with my eyes, I trust that the current knows where it is going. I shall let go, and let it take me where it will." The other creatures laughed and said, "Fool... Let go and that current you worship will throw you tumbled and smashed across the rocks.

Yet in time, as the creature refused to cling, the current lifted him free from the bottom. He was bruised and hurt no more."

Richard Bach in his book, *Illusions* reminds me that resistance is my biggest dis-ease. By resisting the contrast I face every day, I give it the power to control my life. It becomes a lifestyle; fighting against this or that to prove that I am right and justified. I find myself in a group of fears where each action demands an equal act of retaliation. I live in an underworld of blame and shame where vengeance is the motto of existence. I am a creature that clings to confused thoughts that create a life of fear and pain. I do it to comply with what I have been taught and how I feel about myself. I must fight against everything in order to win, but what is the prize for the victory; a life of separation and judgment where I hide from myself by transferring my weakness to others and call it strength? The only thing I feel is loneliness and I use my power to make myself helpless.

As Bach points out I live in a current—a current of consciousness that is filled with love. By resisting the contrast instead of accepting and working with it, I sink in an undertow of fearful thoughts. The world becomes the undertow and all I see and feel is misery. When I release these thoughts and allow the current to take me with it, I am connected to the energy that is life; I am a whole part of another whole that flows endlessly in wellness.

Now reconnected to who I am, I live without doubts. I know all I experience is there for my benefit, not my destruction. This stream of energy runs through everything I see or imagine. My dreams are a workshop filled with tools of learning; I just need to use and appreciate them for what they are—another reality. Every tick of the clock is a reminder that I am here to grow and expand, not to shrink and conform. I am a creature who expresses himself in creation; I only need awareness to flow with the current of love and become its expression.

The choice is mine. I can stay on the bottom and cling to the thoughts that keep me there, or I can release myself and float with the current in an endless stream of abundance that offers everything and expects nothing but the power of positive thinking. That current is ALL THERE IS and ALL I NEED to be free and cling-less like the creature I thought I would be—the creature who believes in the power of consciousness.

2. A Form of Formlessness

No single thing abides, but all things flow.
Fragment to fragment clings; the things thus grow
Until we know and name them. By degrees
They melt, and are no more the things we know.
Globed from the atoms falling slow or swift
I see the suns, I see the system lift
Their forms; and even the systems and their suns
Shall go back slowly to the eternal drift.
Thou too, O Earth—thine empires, lands and seas—
Least, with thy stars, of all the galaxies,
Globed from the drift like these, like these thou too
Shall go. Thou art going, hour by hour, like these.
Nothing abides. The seas in delicate haze
Go off; those mooned sands forsake their place;
And where they are shall other seas in turn
Mow with their scythes of whiteness other bays.

Lucretius was born in 99 BC and was a Roman poet and
philosopher. Not much is known about him except his epic
work of philosophical poetry called "De Rerum Natura, On
the Nature of Things." The poem above is from that work as
paraphrased by Mallock.

I find Lucretius's words as timely today as they were
misunderstood back then. In this world of form and matter all
things will flow back to formlessness. This concept has been
written about and studied for centuries and we certainly see
it happening every minute in nature—the nature that we are
connected to, not separate from.

It has been the topic of life and the quest of humanity to create this formlessness in its own image. Each of us has our own idea of what this experience will bring, and how we will accept it. It does have different names, unique circumstances and fearful ideas depending on who or what is creating this other existence.

One thing is certain; we all go back to the eternal drift, but drifting where, and drifting how? In all languages and in all religions the answer is the same, I return to love. This is the love I never left but forgot in order to be a grander version of oneness; to express and expand myself in physical form in order to expand my formlessness; the formlessness of love. I remember the other aspects of my consciousness that are me. They dwell in other dimensions yet I connect to them. In unity with my Source I become what I am, a whole part of the whole of ALL THERE IS.

Lucretius explains this source of all life in his words below:

Thou, O, Venus, art sole mistress of the nature of things, and without thee nothing rises up into the divine realms of life, nothing grows to be lovely or glad... Through all the mountains and the seas and the rushing rivers, and the leafy nests of birds, and the plains of bending grass, thou strikest all breasts with fond love, and drivest each after its kind to continue its race of through hot desire... For so soon as the spring shines upon the day, the wild herd bound over the happy pastures, and swim the rapid streams, each imprisoned by thy charms, and following thee with desire.

I hear this message and live it through my thoughts. I experience the beauty of love through my acts of service. I express the essence of love in my words and actions. I become the nature of love, by believing I am love, and by sharing myself in gratitude. I am a form of formlessness, following my desire to be a spirit having a human experience.

3. An Island or a Continent?

Coming into feeling—bringing mind into the body—on the one hand gives us the experience we call life. On the other hand, it provides each of us with a sense of loneliness and separation from all others. We must learn to see that we are still one. We may appear to ourselves as islands, but we form a continent of life.

Fred Alan Wolf, PhD explains the nature of existence in this physical world. It appears that I am an uninhabited island floating in a sea of mystery, where there are storms and waves of consciousness that wash over my shores. Unaware of what this consciousness can be, I feel the effects of the waves but allow them to return to the sea of mystery. Every second a new wave enters my mind in the form of thought. I accept it as something expected, but I have no idea why it manifested in the first place. Often these thoughts challenge my freedom and hide my truth. I become separated from the sea that provides life and well-being to my creation. Fred puts it this way:

The illusion that mind and matter are mechanically separate may cause needless human suffering. Grasping for security will never cease as long as we think of the world as only material and fail to realize our own operational thoughts and actions within it. Perhaps the realization that mind and matter cannot be separated— that they are aspects, much like sides of a single coin, of one and only one greater yet subtler reality— will enable the twenty-first century to be born in an atmosphere of peace not yet attainable.

My thoughts affect everything. They are a form of consciousness that manifests into matter. Thus, matter creates the world as I know it, and I live according to the blueprint I follow in physical form. When I awaken to the fact that this blueprint overlaps and connects with all other forms of matter, I begin to see the mystery for what it is—a sea of remembering, not separation. With new awareness I can create a life filled with peace and love. I feel the rocks of unity that attach me to the sea and I welcome the storms of consciousness as gifts from another island. I become the sea itself and bask in the sun of freedom.

Fred continues: *"It bears repeating: Matter arises from mind—a vast field of influence commonly envisioned as the Mind of God."*

My thoughts, my consciousness is a whole part of this great field of influence and I have the ability to create a world filled with the essence of this field and live in harmony with it. It is my choice and my time to feel the energy that runs through me and around me. I am an island on the surface but I am connected to the continent of love beneath the waves of pain. I can live and accept the pain knowing that I am expanding into a grander version of the island created by love.

My thoughts float freely in the sea and I build a temple of awareness that knows not only matter, but also the spirit that creates it. Time drifts off into the horizon and I am a bird of paradise resting on the shore of my inhabited island, singing a song of silence that is in sync with all life.

4. Does a Pebble Ever Die?

Clouds are flowing in the river; waves are flying in the sky.
Life is laughing in a pebble.
Does a pebble ever die?
Flowers grow out of garbage, such a miracle to see.
What seems dead and what seems dying
Makes for butterflies to be.
Life is laughing in a pebble,
Flowers bathe in morning dew,
Dust is dancing in my footsteps
And I wonder who is who.
Clouds are flowing in the river,
Clouds are drifting in my tea,
On a never-ending journey,
What a miracle to be!

Eveline Beumkes is a Dutch poet and author living in Amsterdam. Her work above captures the essence of life. Miracles surround me, the consciousness of a flower or a pebble is not real to me until I become real.

In each form of life there is purpose and growth. Whatever I experience is a lesson in the college of physical being. I learn about myself and then teach what I have learned through my actions. There is no report card—no passing or failing grade. It is my feelings that graduate into a grander version of who I am.

A few years ago at a dinner with friends in Florida, I was talking about my day-to-day encounters with rocks. I had been building walkways around my property and was using rocks I found scattered about. In the process of building this path, I realized something about the rocks that I had never paid any attention to before. Each one was different. Each had its own minerals and fossils that made it the shape it had become. They all had unique qualities of size, shape, weight and color. Some of their shapes resembled the heads of animals or certain states. Some were filled with ancient sea shells from oceans that once filled the land upon which I stood. Every rock I touched, had its own "feeling," and I began to sense that feeling within me. I discovered that these inanimate objects were a form of consciousness.

I explained this to my friends and as you might suspect, they thought I had been in the sun too long and my mind was a bit distorted. I did my best to make them aware of the beauty I found in rocks and what they were teaching me, but the conversation changed to the wine we were drinking that night. As Eveline asks, does a pebble ever die? I think not. It may change in size or color and it might even change its location, but consciousness lives in the web of ALL THERE IS.

The rocks that helped me build my "Path to Nowhere," became a grander version of what they are. They now perform a service and sit in a row of beauty. I may have been the energy that helped them in their quest for growth, but they sit in perfect silence, just being. I call this co-creation in physical form. I call this expansion of the universe. I call this a reason for being a spirit having a human experience.

5. Every Now of It

We live in a river of time in which the source of the river (our past) and its final destination ahead of us (our future) already exists. In what I call "the new alchemy," the future decides the present and the past falls under the control of the present! In other words, the future includes the waves of unpopped possibilities and the past record of popped actualities. However, it is always possible to undo the popping and re-create the past.

Wow! That's interesting reading. I never focused on the river of time that way. Dr. Fred Alan Wolfe, the quantum physicist, wrote that statement in his book, *Dr. Quantum's Little Book of Big Ideas*. What he is saying is that I can change the past and I can pick my present by choosing probabilities from my future. In fact, that's how I got to this point in the river of time. Dr. Wolfe goes on to say:

Think of the future as a series of pictures of yourself. Each picture portrays a different you, much as an actor changes his guise with makeup and mannerism. Each of these futures lives in time ahead of us just as our neighbors live in the space around us. Each friendly "neighbor" calls to us, perhaps over the backyard fence or on the telephone, and invites us over. We must choose whom to visit.

Now that seems far-fetched, based on the information I have been given by my educational institutions. But, after rereading and thinking about his words, there is something inside of me that already knows what Dr. Wolfe is talking about. I just had to see it to remember it. I do pick my future without realizing what I am doing. I do live my present from thoughts that come from my future, and my past is sitting within me now, in this present. So, when I hear the term, "living in the now is all there is," I begin to realize that the past and future are here in this present moment of now. I begin to discover that life in the river of time is now and only now.

Of course it takes an adjustment in my thinking to get to that point. I have been trained to worry about the future, feel guilty about the past and unsure about my present. All these thoughts are based on fear and separation—a reality created by my thoughts and the thoughts of others. I see myself as a victim of this system and struggle to find peace and security within it. My ego swims in this river with the life jacket of hate tied around me, but I call it love. My head sinks below the surface of the river because I don't know how to swim in the freedom of the river, and I drown in my own reality. Day by day I try to keep my head above water, but my thoughts of separation pull me under.

Dr. Wolfe's ideas are not new. They have been written about in the past as well as the future. My ego consciousness is beginning to understand what has been present forever. Now is the point in the river when I begin to experience what I know innately. Now is life, filled with the excitement of creating a joyful, abundant existence by believing I can. Now is the moment of truth when I allow the energy of my Source to guide me through the river wrapped in love and happiness. Now is the essence of ALL THERE IS and I am connected to it in the web of the past, present and future.

The river of time keeps flowing. It takes me to the place I never left and I enjoy every now of it!

6. History Smiles

Why should not we also enjoy an original relation to the universe? Why should not we have a poetry and philosophy of insight and not of tradition, and a religion by revelation to us, and not the history of theirs? Embosomed for a season in nature, whose floods of life stream around and through us, and invite us, by the powers they supply, to action proportioned to nature, why should we grope among the dry bones of the past?

Ralph Waldo Emerson was born in 1803 in Massachusetts, was a graduate from Harvard and a Unitarian minister. He was also a poet, philosopher and author. He was godfather for William James. He influenced Thoreau, was friends with Walt Whitman, Nathaniel Hawthorne, Samuel Coleridge, and Thomas Carlyle. He was considered a leader in the transcendental movement of the early nineteenth century. His work continues to be an important source of inspiration for writers everywhere. His quote above brings up some interesting ideas. Are we, as he said, captured by the past? And, do we live our lives based on the principals of others? Does history think for us instead of it being what it is—a path that got us where we are now?

Certainly history is important. It does repeat itself, adding new bits of information as we rediscover it. What Emerson said in 1840 was certainly foreign to group thinking at that time, but what about now? Realizing that my thoughts create my world and how I perceive it in all aspects of my life is not a silly idea. In fact, science has given this fact its nod of approval. I do have direct control over how and what I believe. That includes everything I perceive. If I want to live by my own truth, not the often-distorted truths of history, I am fulfilling my journey. If I want to see the world as peaceful and abundant, that is my prayer. If I want to create a life of joy, laughter, and love, that is my mission. Nothing can do that for me.

Diversity of thought has been history's trademark. It has stimulated and created love as well as war, hatred, and judgment. I can pick what I want to bring with me on my journey and incorporate it in my life, but what about nature? Emerson knew that nature's history is now. It is showing us how to live. No past wars or injustices; no distorted religious or political beliefs to learn. Just experience the essence of consciousness now. We have the ability to be who we are and to share our truth in unity while accepting diversity as the tool for growth, not destruction. Nature and I repeat ourselves in a cycle of awareness. My history is in the trees and animals, the mountains and the oceans. My history is now, smiling at me.

7. Got A Match?

Since then, at an uncertain hour, that agony returns: And till my ghastly tale is told, this heart within me burns.

That thought, written by Coleridge in *The Rime of the Ancient Mariner*, sounds like we all have a deep burning inside that is trying to let something out and release ourselves. This burning is different things to different people based on life experiences. Some of us may have more agony than others. Some keep the fire burning within and slowly deep fry on the inside.

We could control our fire if we knew why it was burning in the first place. Why is there so much pent up energy lurking within us? Why do we explode over seemingly unimportant things and remain cool in the eye of a major storm? Each one of us has our own personal drama and each story line is unique. My ignition button is set at a different frequency than yours; we both have similar experiences that make us react in drastically different ways and times. Within all this different sameness, we try to find answers to the same questions. The questions are posed in various forms and the answers are revealed in all sorts of information. One man's quest for freedom from himself may be my demise. Survival is measured by how I perform based on averages. If I keep my fire burning at the same strength as everyone else, I'm okay, right? If I explode at the same time as everyone else, then I'm okay, right? Suddenly it's not about me anymore. It's about everybody else, and that is where I get trapped.

Internal fires or pent up energy are all created by my thoughts. I have chosen to use the energy that comes into my body, and channel it to my cells and organs. If I block the energy from flowing freely through my system, using distorted or negative thoughts, I start gathering matchsticks for my fire. The more sticks I gather, the more chance there is to create a fire. One day a major blockage occurs and the sticks burst into flames. I feel uneasy, nervous, tense and angry. I can't control my thoughts; they want me to add more fuel to the fire. I continue to burn inside, until I blow up. Nothing makes sense except the heat of uncontrolled emotions. It's like the hurricane that doesn't care where it hits it just hits something.

After the flames die, the fire's out, and I feel better. I calm myself in forgiveness and understanding. I realize that I started the fire and created the explosion. From that pain, I can begin to heal if I see the lesson and growth it offers. There is no reason to explode again, unless I choose to put myself through that experience. My goal is to not start a fire in the first place. I can always smell the smoke before a major fire and I can use my emotions to extinguish it. Awareness of my feelings and emotions will guide me in releasing energy through the internal system that is part of who I am.

I am Smokey the Bear. It is up to me to prevent my internal fire from becoming a five-alarm life tragedy and living in misery.

8. *House Made of Dawn*

The first thing in the morning I like to give thanks to the universe, to my source, and to all life for the day ahead. It gives me a great feeling of unity to know that I will express myself in the now in a way I had not done before. Gratitude brings well-being. Forgiveness brings connection to my thoughts. It is a treat to feel myself in that way.

The Navajo people were an ancient people in spirit. They gave thanks to everything they saw. They knew and felt their connection to all life and were grateful for the opportunity to live surrounded by natural beauty. How fortunate they were to know the universe inside of them. How fortunate am I to be able to learn from them. They did not need the influence of religion or democracy to worship a God; they were living examples of the God in all of us.

I found this Navajo prayer and will use it in my daily thanks from now on. In its simplicity, it says everything. It gives thanks for my home, my health, my surroundings and my happiness in a beautiful way. What a wonderful way to start each day!

Navajo Chant

House made of dawn.
House made of evening light.
House made of dark cloud.
House made of male rain.
House made of dark mist.
House made of female rain.
House made of pollen.
House made of grasshoppers.
Dark cloud is at the door.
The trail out of it is dark cloud.

The zigzag lightning stands high upon it.
An offering I make.
Restore my feet for me.
Restore my legs for me.
Restore my body for me.
Restore my voice for me.
This very day take out your spell for me.
Happily I recover.
Happily my interior becomes cool.
Happily I go forth.
My interior feeling cool, may I walk.
No longer sore, may I walk.
Impervious to pain, may I walk.
With lively feelings, may I walk.
As it used to be long ago, may I walk.
Happily may I walk.
Happily, with abundant dark cloud, may I walk.
Happily, with abundant showers, may I walk.
Happily, with abundant plants, may I walk.
Happily, on a trail of pollen, may I walk.
Happily may I walk.
Being as it used to be long ago, may I walk.
May it be beautiful before me.
May it be beautiful behind me.
May it be beautiful below me.
May it be beautiful above me.
May it be beautiful all around me.
In beauty it is finished.
In beauty it is finished.

9. Just Let the Creativity Flow

When we speak of nature it is wrong to forget that we are ourselves a part of nature. We ought to view ourselves with the same curiosity and openness with which we study a tree, the sky or a thought, because we too are linked to the entire universe.

Henri Matisse was born in 1869. Certainly all of us have been exposed to him through his art. Henri's life inspires me. I have his self-portrait painted in 1937 hanging on the wall in my studio. Of course it's an unsigned print, but it doesn't matter. He hangs there quietly inspiring my work. Henri sees the beauty in all life. And, and as you can see, he felt connected to the all of the universe.

In studying many artists and writers, I find that feeling of connectedness expressed through their work. Unity with all life and an awareness of how we play a part in it has been the topic of creativity for centuries, and with good reason. It's teaching us to remember. Once I realized I didn't have to be a renowned visionary in some field of endeavor to be creative, my field of vision changed.

It seems our educational system puts levels and restrictions on creativity, and I got lost in the system of believing I wasn't creative. I felt like I couldn't draw, my writing was not accepted, and I had no musical ability other than knowing good music when I heard it. All these beliefs lead me to the conclusion that I was not creative. I measured my accomplishments by others, and their opinions shaped what I thought of myself. Boy, how did I ever get into that trap?

Well, I did get out of the trap and know that I am creative and have always taken part in the creation of my life. Whether or not I am recognized by my actions, I still create how I live each day. I become what I create. We all have different beliefs and those beliefs create how each of us lives. I am not here to change any one's beliefs; the believer must change them, but I can share what I believe.

My life is lived by my thoughts and desires and they are as unique as the consciousness of a dog, or a fly, or a plant, we are all connected. Living matter joined in the performance of nature, each one of us expressing a God within ourselves in different ways. How beautiful is this symphony of life and the instruments that play the music. The creativity that exists as I look around my world is astonishing. I live in tandem with such diversity and beauty, that my thoughts overflow with creativity and gratitude. I am connected to a web of creativity that is part of ALL THERE IS, which is greater than all of these parts.

Love in endless creation, expanding in the mixture of all consciousness and changing as it grows; perfect but moving towards a greater perfection within infinity.

My friend Henri knew this and he was able to tap into the intuitive knowledge we all have stored within us. He expressed that knowledge through his paintings and sometimes through writing. He mentioned this intuitiveness to his students. *"First of all you must cut off your tongue because your decision to paint takes away from your right to express yourself with anything but your brush."*

Pure expression is our purpose. We are learning to be a grander version of our creations. We just have to let it flow.

10. We Belong To Each Other

If we have no peace, it is because we have forgotten we belong to each other.

Those words from Mother Teresa can be thought about in many different ways. Certainly, we all have a sense of belonging. That fact is apparent in our families, friends, churches, and business structures. It really is important to belong to someone or something; for it gives us the comfort of knowing we are not in this life drama alone. We have a physical connection with others who are similar to ourselves that brings us love, laughter, and rewards, as well as anger, pain, and judgment. We balance all these emotions within our individual consciousness and project our own type of peace into our world. We take a great deal of satisfaction in knowing that we have made peace with all those immediately around us. Our lives have purpose. We have a sense of unity.

I took part in a writer's teleconference last night, and there were some technical difficulties that prevented the moderator to hook into the call. Graciously, one of the other participants took over the conference, and tried to help connect the person who was having problems getting in. Most of the people on the call (about 20) didn't know each other personally; we had each read something the others had written, but that was all we knew of each other. When the temporary moderator tried to get our original leader connected, the rest of us on the call were disconnected, and it happened twice. Rather than being frustrated, annoyed or angry about the situation, each participant called back to continue the conference. On the third attempt, our original moderator was on the line and we began our discussion. We had a wonderful meeting and learned some things that would have been missed if we had not called back.

Here we were—a group of strangers for the most part, wanting to connect and have this feeling of belonging just to learn and do it peacefully. We belonged to each other and shared our well-being in the form of writing. We had formed a new family so to speak. We had a sense of togetherness.

Mother Teresa knew what she meant when she said those words. She looked at the larger picture of who we are, and how we treat each other. It is easier to belong to the ones closest to you, but what about those we don't seem to understand? Those we are in physical conflict with.

We do belong to them, just as much as the strangers I met last night. We resolved our differences in communication peacefully, and learned from the experience. We learned something new about each other and formed a respect that will continue as we grow. Just by thinking outside our range of comfort, we change our world. We live to share ourselves in gratitude and love. We begin to remember who we really are. We have the peace that Mother Teresa had and continues to share.

11. Who is Living Life?

*And yet, though we strain against the deadening grip of daily
necessity, I sense there is this mystery. All life is being lived.
Who is living it, then? Is it the things themselves, or something
waiting inside them, Like an unplayed melody in a flute? Is it
the wind blowing over the waters? Is it the branches that signal
to each other? Is it flowers interweaving their fragrances, or
streets, as they wind through time? Is it the animals warmly
moving, or the birds, that suddenly rise up? Who lives it then?
God, are you the one who is living life?*

Rainer Maria Rilke asks some great questions in his poem
"Who Is Living Life?" Who is living this life I call my own; or
any life that I call alive?

Life is in everything. Life is consciousness. Is my connection
with all life the fact that a common otherness is living through
all things and me? I can't understand it with my physical tools,
my 5 senses, yet it is there within me with no shape or texture
but it is guiding me with a fluid feeling of well-being. Am I the
same as it is, but totally unaware of my connection? Can I be
united with all things by being in love with myself? Not ego
love, but the love that cannot be measured by words or symbols.
Can I feel the magic of creation surrounding me and swallowing
me in pure awareness? Will I allow myself the thought that God
is within me?

I can answer those questions by feeling my emotions; by seeing
unity in life without separation by sharing my love of self
with all in gratitude, and by knowing that the otherness in
me is living this life in order to grow and expand in this
expanding universe.

By believing in the web of ALL THERE IS, I can answer Rilke
by saying: "Yes, the God in me is the one who is living life."

12. Silence

The pause, that impressive silence, that eloquent silence, that geometrically progressive silence, which often achieves a desired effect where no combination of words, howsoever felicitous could accomplish it.

Mark Twain, was born in 1835, and enjoyed an illustrious career as a writer, humorist and all around great mind. He had a way with words, and as you see from this quote understood silence as well.

Silence has been written about for centuries. It has a special quality of being there when you need it, or not being there to understand it. Silence has the distinct ability to defy definition. Silence is never silent, only wordless. Within silence, another world takes shape. In speechlessness, my mind is not silent, yet there is silence. In dreams there is silence, but I am far from being silent. Silence is everywhere, in everything, and is often misunderstood.

It can mean indifference, insanity, insecurity, stupidity, and even genius. Of course, silence doesn't care about any of that; it continues with or without my judgments. It seems within space there is silence, but now science has discovered it is anything but silent.

So what is this silence? What is this thing of thinglessness? I know I can't function without it, yet sometimes it's hard to function with it. Silence is, just as I am. It is the glue that holds my world together. Someone once said, "Moments of silence are a part of the music." It is part of my music—part of who I am. In a minute's silence, I can accomplish more than days full of noise. In silence, I am connected to my Source. In silence, I become silently blended into the harmony of ALL THERE IS.

The "Ancient Boy" Lao-tzu says it this way:

Thirty spokes are made one by holes in a hub
By vacancies joining them for a wheel's use
The use of clay in molding pitchers
Comes from the hollow of its absence;
Doors, windows, in a house,
Are used for their emptiness:
Thus we are helped by what is not
To use what is.

Words, the symbols we use for thought, can't capture the essence
of an experience. Silence is such a word. Within its emptiness
lies an unexplored world waiting for discovery. I only need
to focus on silence to experience and express it. In doing so, I
become it.

—

Joy

1. Am I Really Full of BS?

At the dawn of eternal love, souls fly out of bodies and man
reaches the stage of perception where with every breath he can
see and touch without eyes and without hands.

Rumi the thirteenth century mystic, poet and theologian reminds
me that I have more awareness when I experience the love that
is within me. Once I release the true nature of my being
without restrictions, I can begin to see and touch without my
eyes or hands. My feelings are my senses and they never lie.
My emotions are my guidance system and once I align them
with my truth, they never lie.

There was a little book that became popular a couple of years ago.
It was written by the renowned moral philosopher from Princeton
University Harry Frankfurt. It is titled *On Bullshit*. Dr. Frankfurt
pointed out that everything I say and do has the element of "BS"
connected to it. From good morning statements, work situations,
family interaction, simple daily conversation, and even dealing
with myself, all have a certain amount of BS in them.

Why is that? That's how the system works. No one should reveal
the real person resting within their physical form. It seems that
little lies don't hurt anyone or anything. It's no one's business
anyway, right? Besides, who knows? That "BS" could get me a
job, or a wife, or money and fame. I don't have to be 100 percent
honest to be successful. Who is?

All I have to do is look at the news to see where this BS has
gotten us: wars, political nightmares, social injustice, poverty,
killing and a general feeling of disconnection. The Truth is not
a truth at all. It's filled with BS that I overlook, because I think
that is the way I should live. My world and I are floating in a
stream of BS that is stinking up my life and my perceptions.

I can change all of that by believing my own truth. My truth is that I am love, connected to ALL THERE IS, which is love. Love is only good. There is no opposite. It does not live in the duality of time and space. It brings me all I need, if I allow it, if I let it flow in the brook of my truth. I can then deal with each physical event with love, speaking and acting with feelings and true emotions. My truth knows no fear, so I can be free to express myself in joy.

I can be the change I want to see in my world. In love, everything changes to love. My thoughts become my truth. I am the dawn of eternal love that Rumi talks about. I see and touch my world without eyes and hands. I walk the same path every day, but I see a whole new world around me—a world that is filled with my truth.

Maybe by eliminating that little white lie, we really could change the world.

2. Am I Having Fun Yet?

Nothing is at last sacred but the integrity of your own mind.

Emerson said a lot in that short sentence. It seems I have overlooked the power I have within my reach. My thoughts create my experiences and also create what I want to look like. I can have fun all the time, if I believe I can.

Fun means different things to me. Fun could be a vacation from my daily activities, perhaps a trip or just sitting with nature for a few hours. Exercise is fun, when I realize I like it. Understanding the benefits that exercise brings me is fun. It seems I don't have fun, if my body looks different than I think it should. The weight trap certainly takes a toll on fun. It's not fun looking at myself with judgmental eyes and a helpless attitude. My mental mirror creates a distorted view, based on what others look like. Others can't change my opinion of my form, unless I change first. What do I want to look like? Skinny, fat, or within the weight limits of some chart? Perhaps, I want to look like someone I'm not. Do I want to look like another me longing to accept another reality?

What I really want is to look like fun. I want to bring that emotional well-being to my physical form. I want to treat myself to loving thoughts, accepting friends, and exciting events. I want to open myself to the wonders of physical life and face each moment in truth. I want to see all the grandeur within me, so I can give and share it with all life. I want to treat myself with respect and understanding so my weight is no longer a sign of weakness. I want to feed my world with laughter and kindness, so I see myself in others. I want to fuel myself with pure energy from my Source. Food for thought will be the first food I choose. It is no longer a crutch or obsession unless I want it to be.

I create my physical form by choice: fun or suffering. I want to look at myself as love, connected to love and I want to remember who I am. My spirit has no weight. Consciousness is not dense, but fluid. Weightlessness is my original state of time. Fun is my original state of mind.

3. A Pack Rat of Love

My Hobby

I collect rainbows after a thundershower. They're rare!
I collect authentic winks from beautiful women.
I collect warm handshakes from complete strangers.
I'm always, every day and every night, on the look-out for a smile.
I collect the sound of laughter. Not really as plentiful as they
used to be.
I collect mean expressions. I have so many now; I'm ready to
trade for other things.
I collect "Thank yous" and phrases like "I'll never forget you,"
or "You've made my day!"
I collect postcards with scenes that don't exist anymore.
I have a huge collection of pain, but seldom refer to it. Like it or
not, it is one heck of a part of my collection. Funny thing about
pain, it's hard to trade or unload.
I collect the expressions of kitties or puppies. Wish I could
collect that smell that goes along with them.
I collect sunsets and sunrises. You say they're always the same?
Wrong!
I collect the look of patients in hospitals. Sometimes, I swear, no
matter what has happened to them, what their color or sex is,
they all seem to look and sound the same.
I feel sorry for people who don't have a hobby, who don't
collect anything! How many times have you heard in life,
"There are a lot of things I'd like to collect, but I can't afford it!"
or "I don't have the money, it's as simple as that!"
The one thing we can all collect, the least expensive and perhaps
the most rewarding of all is our memories.
Have I missed certain things that I should have collected and didn't?
Sure! It's the one hobby remaining, the rarest hobby since
the beginning! Not one of us can say our collection is complete

without it. It's the one thing none of us can find in an antique shop, a gallery, alongside the Nile, off the Great Barrier Reef, at the peak of Everest or at the bottom of the ocean's floor—TIME!

Jonathan Winters was born in 1925 and is one of America's greatest comics. His essay above came from his book *Winters' Tales*.

Collecting things has been a hobby of mine for years. My wife calls me a pack rat. Well she's got a point; I really didn't need any of the stuff I found precious and had to have. In fact, it became more of a burden than a joy, so I began to get rid of the clutter I had built around me. Being a collector, I just couldn't stop cold turkey, so I began collecting some of the things Jonathan talks about instead; smiles and hugs, magic memories, friends, and most of all love. I don't need a special room or garage for my collections now, they follow me wherever I go and I can spend time with them whenever I want. They have no monetary value but have exceptional spiritual worth; they fill my heart with gratitude.

In a way, I am collecting the "time" that Jonathan says we all want and desire, because my collectibles are with me in the now. I have packaged them in my thoughts and they have become timeless. I am always looking for new things to collect and every day I find a new treasure to cherish and enjoy. My wife now calls me a pack rat of love.

4. A Sneerless World

From her book, *The Pathwork of Self-Transformation*," Eva Pierrakos writes, *"It is not the world outside yourself that confuses you; it is the world within your own consciousness that does so."*

That makes a lot of sense when I study how I shape my life with my thoughts. Certainly confusion starts within me and spreads outward, not the other way around. The separation of consciousness creates confusion and I begin to base my life on those thoughts. The events created are from one aspect of my consciousness and I experience an uncomfortable existence. Fred Alan Wolf Ph.D explains it this way:

Life is a series of punctuated conscious moments. Much like the frames of a motion picture on a reel passing through a projector create an image and then vanish, our awareness of life also passes from instant to instant.

Every action we take involves this kind of on-off movement. Each time we raise an eyebrow in incredulity, or flare our nostrils in a sneer, a large number of mental events occur. As we listen to an untrustworthy politician's speech, not all of our neurons, muscle fibers, skin patched, and nerve endings want to go along to produce our incredulous sneer. Some of these bodily components, undoubtedly, want to laugh or even inhibit the actions of the other components composing the sneer. But, the homeostatic majority usually wins because it not only outweighs the minority, it also can enforce its behavior in more and different ways than can our hetero static behavior modifications.

In a society of sneerers, your sneer is expected. You have learned well how to sneer. You have watched your peers sneer. You have learned just how to hold your head, to flare your nostrils, and to condescend. The society of sneerers could conceivably encompass a whole country! In such a country, perhaps sneering becomes an accepted, expected norm, and if we lived in that country perhaps our normal expression would be "sneerful." Thus, our faces become the face of a nation. Not only that, but our way of speaking may be shaped by our faces, our expressions literally shaping the very way we utter a word. What would have to occur to create a shift from a sneer to a grin? Awareness and intent.

Fred explains Eva's statement in an understandable way. I do create the confusion I live in. I do express myself through my words and actions and confusion reigns in my daily life. I sneer and worry about the things I created in order to be accepted in a "sneerful world." There is another part of me that does not want to be sneerful. It sits within me grinning, patiently waiting for me to wake up and change my intent.

The world I choose to live in can be filled with abundance, happiness, and peace. I am the projector that plays the film of life. Within me lies the limitless library of universal consciousness that is filled with infinite possibilities. Free will enables me to choose what I want to experience; it enables me to be united in thought, and function as a whole connected to another whole. Knowing I can be more than a sneer brings me joy; it brings me comfort and it brings me back to ALL THERE IS—love with a grin.

5. A Sweat Shop or Magic Shop?

Work is love made visible. And, if you cannot work with love, but only with distaste, it is better that you should leave your work and sit at the gate of the temple and take alms of those who work with joy.

Kahlil Gibran was a Lebanese-American artist, poet and writer. Born in Lebanon in 1883, he moved to Boston in 1895. His thoughts and writings influenced a wide variety of people. John Kennedy's famous inaugural speech contained a revised quote from Gibran's book, *The Frontier*, which said, "Are you a politician asking what your country can do for you, or a zealous one asking what you can do for your country."

John Lennon used another altered quote for his song Julia in 1968, *"Half of what I say is meaningless, but I say it so the other half may reach you."*

Kahlil Gibran is best known for his work, *The Prophet*, which has been translated into more than 20 different languages. His quote about work strikes a nerve within me. I never really looked at work as love made visible. I have worked for many years and I must admit many of those years were not filled with love by any definition. I thought more about what it could do for me, and I took advantage of the resources that were placed in front of me. It was more of a burden than an expression of love. I thought it was there for me to abuse, to be angry with and be fearful of. It was rarely a pleasant experience.

My thoughts and beliefs kept me from understanding that the daily work I was performing was an act of love. I made it a place of pain instead.

I did learn the lesson Gibran explains; work is certainly love in full view. It is a service I accept in order to fulfill my desires, and I'm paid for that opportunity. I am able to interact with people in many different situations and learn about diversity. I deal with contrast on a daily basis, and understand how to cope with it. I feel the happiness and joy that accomplishment brings, and I strive to live my life feeling that way. I see myself in the eyes of others and feel the warmth of friendship. Work is a prayer answered when I believe it is. Not for the external rewards alone, but for the growth I give to myself.

I'm working now and all I see is love. All I feel is friendship. All I am is what I see. I do that with my thoughts and beliefs. They make my world either a sweatshop or a magic shop.

In physical life, work is an expression of love. Love is ALL THERE IS when I become it.

6. Boogie to the Bop!

My life flows on in endless song
Above earth's lamentations
I hear the real tho' far off hymn.
That hails a new creation.

Thus all the tumult and the strife,
I hear the music ringing,
It sounds an echo in my soul,
How can I keep from singing?
What tho' the tempest round me roars,
I know the truth it liveth,
What tho' the darkness round me close
Songs in the night it giveth,
No storm can shake my inmost calm,
While to that rock I'm clinging-
Since love is lord of heaven and earth
How can I keep from singing?

"How Can I Keep From Singing" was written by Anne Warner. It was arranged and performed by Pete Seeger. Anne and her husband Frank were renowned collectors, preservers, and interpreters of American traditional folk music. Between 1938 and 1969 they gathered over 1,000 songs and stories. The work above is from those years.

Anne asks a good question. How can I keep from singing in this physical form? I have the song of oneness ringing in my ears and the music of awareness all around me, yet most of the time my voice is filled with everything but an uplifting song. I find myself attached to the dark side of life where the tempest of fear and hate roar inside my mind. Storms of revenge and mistrust cover the melody of daily life and everything and everyone has an agenda that keeps me in a panic. The turmoil of contrast brings

222

me to my knees and I give up and crawl on the lonely path of self-pity. Life is not a song, not even a note, it is an itch that I scratch and open into a wound that bleeds into the stream of unworthiness. Life is not fun; life is a race to the end. I can put myself out of my misery, but all around me I still hear the music.

Ms. Warner knew what that existence was like, and she wrote about it in order to rise above it. She concentrated on the beauty of songs and stories from the heart of our culture and incorporated their messages into her life. She gave her collection of thoughts to the Archive of Folk Culture, so they could be shared and experienced by all of us. By listening to the music, she became a song.

I can be a song. I can be a note of beauty and my melody can float through the air like the clouds. I can dance to the beat of love and waltz through life with grace. The sounds of creation flow through me in an endless song of unity. The rapture of connection beckons a new thought that lifts my spirit with inspiration. I do all this by being who I am. My music is played by a full orchestra that enhances my daily life and touches the souls of those around me.

I am a song. I am the music of love. No storm can change that fact. I am here to sing my song and dance in the garden of dreams. Glorious flowers surround me and I smell the fragrance of lavender as I boogie to the bop of universal consciousness.

7. Come Easy, Go Easy

*I was talking to a moth the other evening. He was trying to
break into an electric light bulb and fry himself on the wires.
Why do you fellows pull this stunt I asked him, because it is
the conventional thing for moths or why if that had been an
uncovered candle instead of an electric light bulb you would
now be a small unsightly cinder. Have you no sense?*

*Plenty of it he answered, but at times we get tired of using it.
We get bored with the routine and crave beauty and excitement.
Fire is beautiful and we know that if we get too close it will
kill us, but what does that matter? It is better to be happy for
a moment and be burned up in beauty, than to live a long time
and be bored all the while, so we wad all our life up into one
little roll, and then we shoot the roll. That is what life is for. It is
better to be part of beauty for one instant and then cease to exist,
than to exist forever and never be a part of beauty. Our attitude
toward life is come easy, go easy. We are like human beings used
to be before they became too civilized to enjoy themselves.*

~ Archy

That is from the work of Don Marquis. He created Archy, the
cockroach and Mehitabel, the cat, who left poems on his
typewriter by jumping on the keys. Don was born in 1878 in
Illinois and became an author, newspaper columnist, poet, artist,
and as you can see humorist. He wrote 35 books, drew cartoons
for the New Yorker Magazine and wrote columns for the New
York Sun and Saturday Evening Post. In 1943, the US Navy
launched the USS Don Marquis in tribute to him.

Don says a lot about how I think. It is easy to hide from beauty
by not thinking about it, or by thinking that beauty is something
foreign to me. There is always something more beautiful,
more appealing, and more exciting than the life I create.

Somehow beauty becomes a desire, rather than an innate trait. So, the search begins to attract beauty into my life by acquiring things and establishing my dominance over my fellow man and my external world. Just like the moth, I seek beauty with fire in my eyes and excitement in my quest. But the beauty I seek eludes me, and I wander through life too civilized to enjoy the gift I have within me.

The moth had it right when he said that finding beauty for a moment is worth a lifetime of searching. I am beauty if I think I am. I experience what I think. I'm able to express my beauty in my words and actions and give my beauty to all life. Then, I become my desire and expand in joy.

Beauty can come easy, if I allow it. Beauty can go easy, if I give it to all I meet. Beauty can be civilized if I enjoy who I am.

8. Convulsive Respiration

There is a species of primate in South America more gregarious than most other mammals with a curious behavior. The members of this species often gather in groups, large and small. In the course of their mutual chattering, under a wide variety of circumstances, they are induced to engage in bouts of involuntary, convulsive respiration, a sort of loud, helpless, mutual reinforcing group panting that sometimes is so severe as to incapacitate them. Far from being adverse; however, these attacks seem to be sought out by most members of the species, some of whom appear to be addicted to them. We might be tempted to think that if only we knew what it was like to be them, from the inside, we'd understand this curious addiction of theirs. If we could see it "from their point of view," we could know what it was for. But in this case we can be quite sure that such insight as we might gain would still leave matters mysterious. For we already have the access we seek; the species is Homo sapiens (which does indeed inhabit South America, among other places), and the behavior is laughter.

That quote belongs to Daniel C. Dennett, an Oxford educated philosopher as he explains laughter in his book *Consciousness Explained*, published in 1991.

Laughter is the exercise we all need and never get enough of. It is what makes us realize who we are. I always feel a surge of energy going through my body after a good laugh, and I always want to be around those who want to laugh. It costs nothing and gives me everything I need to cure what ails me. It's natural healthcare, standard equipment on the human model. I just need to push the button that enables it more often. I have a choice: to feel good, or to feel pain. I know we all want to feel good, but why don't we push the button more often? There are many answers why laughter is not an option. It stems from our

226

thoughts and what we have created in our individual worlds. We do have the ability to change and to enjoy the journey, instead of making it a painful path.

Laughter is the tool that fixes the thought. Laughter is the magic pill of agelessness. Laughter is the drink of unity and the food of awareness. Its benefits have no opposite unless I create them. I can list a lot of things that make me laugh. In fact, life itself is sort of a joke. I convince myself I am something I'm not and then try to live it. That in itself is very funny, but I don't see the humor because I convince myself I'm serious. I see that folly in others and that makes me laugh. Of course the joke is I am really seeing myself.

But all that is changing. I am able to laugh at myself now. I am able to see the humor and enjoyment in being who I am. I am able to look at myself and smile. Life is meant to be filled with laughter—the energy that makes me feel special. A major part of human growth is feeling laughter. I am here to grow into a grander version of myself and laughter is on the list of ingredients that make that happen.

Here's to my next bout of convulsive respiration! May it begin now.

9. Did You Hear the One...

A shoe salesman, who dragged out half his stock to a female customer, asked her, *"Mind if I rest for a few minutes, lady? Your feet are killing me."*

The ability to laugh, especially at ourselves, is part of the prayer arsenal we come physically equipped with at birth. As Ramtha said, *"The greatest prayer you could ever pray would be to laugh every day. For when you do, it elevates the vibratory frequency within your being such that you could heal your entire body."*

True, nothing feels better than laughter, well, almost nothing, but that's another article. Being energy connected to a universe of energy tells me that my vibrations have a lot to do with my overall well-being. Happiness, joy and laughter bring a stream of energy into my systems and send positive messages to my cells. In turn, they function with the energy supplied to them. If I feel good mentally, my body reaps the reward of that sensation. I send that energy to all those around me and they also benefit from what I project. We all know this; that's why we like to be close to people who have a positive energy field around them. We may not see it, but we sure can feel it.

If there was any advice that I remember, it was from my mother who said, "Find some laughter in everything Hon, it will be the vehicle that supports you in any situation. It's not always easy to laugh, but it's there waiting for us to join in."

There have been many situations that I found it hard to laugh about, but at some point I was able to laugh at myself for not being able to see the bright side. Prayer is feeling, and laughter is a part of prayer, for I am able to feel the positive effects within me and around me. The laughter switch, within my body, is always on autopilot, and it only accepts positive vibes. All other sensations need not apply unless I flip my switch.

As the Course in Miracles says, "The world will end in joy because it is a place of sorrow...The world will end in peace, because it is a place for war... The world will end in laughter, because it is a place for tears. Where there is laughter who can longer weep?"

Did you hear the one about being busy? *"I putter, I worry, I push and shove, hunting little molehills to make mountains of."*

Funny and true...

10. *Glowing in Light*

Even if our efforts of attention seem for years to be producing no result, one day a light that is in exact proportion to them will flood the soul.

Simone Weil was born in Paris in 1909. She was a French philosopher and mystic. She died at the age of 34 of anorexia. She developed an interest in healing the social rifts of the masses and providing physical and psychological needs for humanity. Her quote above hints at understanding that the daily experiences I endure do have purpose when I finally realize they do. How and when that happens is based on my thoughts and beliefs.

Simone talks about the light that awakens my soul and changes my thoughts about who I am. That light was there at my birth, but somewhere along my journey it went dark. Every now and then it flickers, as hot coals do, waiting to be lit again. I know now it's never extinguished, I just forgot how to turn up the flame of light.

I search everywhere for the switch that operates my light. I look to others to flick my switch so I can feel my true self, but I still walk in darkness. Most of the time I accept it as natural, this feeling of emptiness and loneliness that pecks at my emotions. Sometimes the peck becomes a bite and I am swallowed by my own fears. I go through the motions of living, but feel a deep hole within me. As the hole gets bigger, my physical body gets weaker and I expose my hole to my world. I become my beliefs and live in the hole instead of remembering my light.

Then it happens, a rogue thought appears from my perceptions, and I stop digging my hole and listen to myself. The thought finds the switch that turns on my light. Another thought changes the bulb, and I become brighter. Then, another thought reconnects my wiring, and my energy is increased by the connection. Another thought shines light on the hole and fills it with pure light. I radiate with the light of awareness. I feel the comfort and love of unity. The emptiness and loneliness are embraced by oneness, and they become love.

Glowing in light, I see my purpose. I remember who I am. I understand my journey and grow and expand in physical and mental form. I offer myself in unconditional universal service to all life and feel my connection to universal consciousness. I live to be a grander version of who I am—a spirit having a human experience and do it in joy.

I see the results of my efforts. I feel my truth. I am love and I share it in gratitude.

11. Harmony of Thoughts

Let us be united,
Let us speak in harmony,
Let our minds apprehend alike.
Common be our prayer,
Common be the end of our assembly,
Common be our resolutions,
Common be our deliberations.
Alike be our feelings,
United be our hearts,
Common be our intentions,
Perfect be our unity.

The Rigveda was written in India over 3000 years ago. The words above are from that work. The text of 1,028 hymns is still in use today at religious functions and various occasions. As I discover these ancient thoughts, I realize how connected we all are and how we ignore that fact with senseless judgment. Everything has a common source, but I call it different names and honor it in different ways to dispute the meaning of life.

Human existence is based on energy and that source of energy is non-judgmental in its disbursement of life forms. All creation comes from one common source. In this world of diversity, I find unity in nature and a common intention of being whole. There is no separation of thought and no judgment of actions in the movement of nature through the rhythm of time. There is no clock to define finality. There is no deceit to hide insecurity and there is no war to gain power over life. There is only a common intention to be truthful in form and unified in spirit.

How did I get the notion that I am so exceptional in my physical life? Why did I assume the role of protector of the universe when there is nothing to protect? I look and feel superior to other forms of life even though they have never lost their connection to their common source. I have developed my own common illusion of separation through misguided beliefs. I destroy life in order to save my own, when in fact there is nothing to save.

The ancients knew how to live in joy. They knew how to appreciate all physical life and unite with it. Unity comes from the knowing that there is no separation; there is no superiority; there is no power greater than the common intention of unity. The desire to be whole within the whole of ALL THERE IS and share its abundance in gratitude is an innate ability directed by my consciousness. I just need to believe in it and release myself in its freedom.

I sit looking out my window and feel the presence of a greater consciousness. I call it many things but it is common in intention, common in feeling, and common in its expansion of my consciousness. I could call it a grander version of myself and I could call it God. Whatever name I use for it, it remains common, united and filled with love. It expands as I remember who I am and what it is.

The words of the Rigveda bring me a little closer to remembering why I am on this physical journey. They fill me with the intention to be united with all life and respect the diversity of thoughts that create the school of learning I find myself immersed in. My beliefs create my world and I will experience those beliefs and express them and then become what I express. I will remember that I am a spirit having a human experience and my intention is to be a grander version of that spirit through uniting myself with all life and enjoying the rewards of being common yet diverse.

12. I'm Framed in Space

One cannot collect all the beautiful shells on the beach. One can only collect a few and they are more beautiful if they are few... Gradually one discards and keeps just the perfect specimen; not necessarily a rare shell, but a perfect one of its kind. One cannot collect all the beautiful shells on the beach. One sets it apart by itself, ringed around by space- like an island. For it is only framed in space that beauty blooms. Only in space are events and objects and people unique and significant-and therefore beautiful. A tree has significance if one sees it against the empty face of the sky. A note in music gains significance from the silences on either side. A candle flowers in the space of night. Even small and casual things take on significance if they are washed in space, like a few autumn grasses in one corner of an Oriental painting, the rest of the page bare. For it is not merely the trivial which clutters our lives but the important as well. We can have a surfeit of treasures-an excess of shells, where one or two would be significant.

Anne Morrow Lindbergh was born in 1906 and was an avid writer and aviation pioneer. She was her husband's radio operator and co-pilot, and was the first woman to be licensed as a glider pilot in the United States. We all know the story of her life and the losses she endured. One of her books, *A Gift from the Sea*, is where the above excerpt can be found.

Anne reminds me that I all I need to do is look around me to see the beauty that fills the space I physically exist in. I need nothing other than my thoughts to feel the significance in everything. I don't need much to appreciate the perfection that continues to unfold before my eyes. One shell holds a treasure of joy, if I allow it and be aware of its message. My world is created by my perceptions and beliefs, and as Lindbergh says, there is surfeit of abundance, waiting for me to experience it. All I need to do is to allow and accept it, and be grateful for the opportunity to express myself in physical form. Everything is there waiting for me to remember. How and when I connect to the beauty in everything is my choice. I have the freedom to become what I believe.

I can collect all the beauty I need by looking within, and then expressing what I feel. My world opens to a space filled with abundance, peace and happiness. It is everywhere I look and is in everything I see, connected in a web of ALL THERE IS, Love.

TM

Harvest

1. A Vessel of Freedom

*Ask someone to give a description of the personality type which
he finds most despicable, most unbearable and hateful, and most
impossible to get along with, and he will produce a description
of his own repressed characteristics—a self description which is
utterly unconscious and which therefore always and everywhere
tortures him as he receives its effect from the other person.*

Edward C. Whitmont was a doctor who offered his patients a
system of healing based on psychology, alchemy, and homeopathy.
He integrated a comprehensive understanding of modern
medicine with quantum physics and ecosystem sciences, such
as Gaia hypothesis and "new story cosmology." Until his death
a few years ago, he was one of the few remaining contemporary
Jungians, who worked directly with C.G. Jung. He was a founding
member of the C.G. Jung training center in New York.

Edward brings up an interesting point about what I hate in
other people. It seems I am always looking for faults in others.
Once they are discovered, a sense of relief engulfs me. I find it
easy to form an opinion of them based on how I feel about myself.
There have been times when I hated the kindness in others,
because I had locked my own kindness in a room of fear.
I questioned other's motives when mine were suspect. I saw their
kindness as a smoke screen because I was behind one. I envied
the success of others because I did not feel worthy of success.
I slowly made myself sick by comparing myself to others in
order to justify my own shortcomings.

Whitmont is telling me that I can eliminate hate by loving myself.
In order to love myself, I must be honest with myself. In order
to be honest, I must forgive myself; a self-confession of
imperfection always releases fears. I am not traveling this path
of remembering to be perfect, but I am traveling to learn from

the contrast I create. All of those hates I see before me are opportunities for me to forgive myself. When I forgive I create ease instead of dis-ease.

There are situations where the anger and emotional upheaval are almost unbearable, that's when I can choose a better thought. I change my attitude by doing something else. I can remove myself from situations that cause me discomfort in order to better understand the lesson I am learning. No one can make me feel bad about myself unless I allow it. I am able to reconnect to my inner wisdom when I focus on it. In just a few minutes I can bring love back into view. All it takes is acceptance.

Hate does not come just from actions; it comes from thoughts that create actions. I can free myself from the illusions of hate and fear by changing the way I feel about myself. I am the one who has that power. My thoughts create the world I see before me; it can be anything and everything I dream of. It can be free from the devastation of anger; free from the judgment of hate; and free from the diseases I fear by believing that I am not alone. I am a whole part of another whole that is connected to a web of ALL THERE IS, Love. In that connection, I am truth, forgiveness, and joy. I see what I feel, and I am a vessel of freedom.

2. To be a Tree!

*Eve bites into the fruit. Suddenly, she realizes that she is naked.
She begins to cry. The kindly serpent picks up a handkerchief
and gives it to her." It's all right," he says, "The first moment is
always the hardest."*

"But, I thought knowledge would be so wonderful," Eve sniffles.

*"Knowledge?" Laughs the serpent. "This fruit is from the Tree of
Life."*

Stephen Mitchell was born in Brooklyn in 1943. He is a poet,
translator, scholar and anthologist. He attended Amherst College,
the University of Paris, and Yale. His work above is titled, *"Into
the Garden."*

The story of Eve is a very famous one indeed. Stephen's poem
brings new life to the story; in fact it brings the Tree of Life
to the story. This Tree has its roots in the physical as well as
spiritual world. It is the prime foundation for wisdom and energy.
It has been written about for centuries. The Jewish Gnostics tell
us, *"Of all things which are both concealed and manifested... the
super celestial fire is the treasure house, as it were a great tree...
from which all things are nourished."*

Trees and the study of this form of consciousness have
fascinated me forever. When I was a kid, I spent many hours
climbing trees and sitting on branches wishing I could fly like
a bird. One day I did, with the help of an airplane. So, that
dream came true. I climbed up and down these life forms and
saw all the life that lived on them and in them and wished they
could tell me about their lives. I sat by the creek that exposed the
roots of a mighty oak and studied the movement of its roots
in order to sustain its form. It was as active below the ground

as it was reaching for the sky. It was two worlds in one, each functioning in its own way in order to grow. I watched the birth of buds on the branches, every one of them holding a mystery soon to be revealed. The burst of leaves signaled the dawn of spring and all of nature seemed to wake up at once. Birds, insects, and animals fill their days enjoying all the energy that the trees shared in unconditional service. These strong elements of nature stand firm and free and express their gratitude in their natural beauty offering shade and food, shelter and warmth, love and gentleness for all who share their world. Peace surrounds them, and awareness defines them. To be a tree was another dream I had.

Just like the tree, I grow in every season. My branches touch life with vibrant energy. I fill myself with thoughts of abundance and I receive all I need. My actions unfold in peace, just like the leaves that open without violence. I find myself rooted in love and nourished by my source in a stream of unified consciousness; just like the roots of my friends, the trees, my nourishment is love.

To Be A Tree

Simple Me

Let Me Be Thee

Said The Flea

3. My Ego Shakes And Wiggles!

"As you move through the inner space of consciousness toward union with Self, there is a bridge you must pass over... It is on this bridge that you shed the remaining particles of error thoughts and negative beliefs and go through the final cleansing. As the bridge comes into view, your world may seem to turn upside down, and the reason is because you are beginning the process of letting go of everything that seemed secure to you... Your ego may choose to do battle as you step on to the bridge, and it will do whatever is necessary to save itself. If that means creating an insufficiency of funds, it will do it, because this effect could very well cause you to step back... Another ego tantrum may give the appearance of a business failure, or the interruption of a successful career, or perhaps a physical ailment. The ego simply wants to show who is boss."

John Price is an author of several books incorporating ancient wisdom, contemporary metaphysics and spiritual philosophy. The quote above is from his book, "The Planetary Commission."

John explains what my first step might feel like when I begin to reconnect to my inner world. After living a life filled with the pleasures of ego-based satisfaction, it's not easy to change my focus. It takes practice, patience and the realization that unity brings wholeness; this wholeness is an awakening of another aspect of who I am. It is the connection I forgot when I began this physical journey.

I have read about the ego and how it controls my everyday life when I allow it to do that. At first it works just fine, then gradually it begins to think for me. My thoughts become fear based ideas and manifest into the world of survival of the strongest; the best, the greatest, the perfect, all live in this world and I strive to become one of them. I'll do anything to be part of the game, even when it starts to destroy me. My ego takes me down the road of breakdowns and I call it life, waiting for death. The road is filled with pain, anger and judgment; and I project those thoughts on to everyone around me; misery attracts company, which is really ego spreading it's inflated sense of worth onto the bread of friendship. At some point other aspects of myself emerge and I begin to wake up.

This awakening comes in many different ways; Pierce explains a few reactions that manifest when I start to question what I am doing with this physical life. These acts of loss represent the bridge of discovery; the illusions disappear and the reality of union takes it place. It's not the death of ego but the marriage of other aspects of consciousness with my ego in order to be the whole that is part of another whole. I begin to see with my feelings and emotions and I sense my connection with all life. I reach within and ring the bell of forgiveness and continue to let it ring; I accept contrast and grow from the lessons it offers me; I open my heart and allow my freedom to shine in the light of diversity.

The union of my inner world is a grand event. I experience things that I never realize existed; I see things for the first time, that were always right in front of me; abundance, happiness and peace fill my thoughts and I express them; I become more than human, I become what I have always been, a spirit having a human experience.

Now I travel my path with unconditional service to all life; I see the beauty in nature and communicate with it; I feel the love that is everything and grow from it; I see separated egos and know that union is just a thought away. My mind becomes a bag filled with the confetti of forgiveness and I continue to reach in the bag and shower myself with this forgiving confetti and spread it freely in gratitude. My ego shakes and wiggles but it remembers now, that it is just a part of the whole that creates my world.

4. The Mouse and the Cheese

I left the woods for as good a reason as I went there. Perhaps it seemed to me that I had several more lives to live, and could not spare any more time for that one... I learned this, at least, by my experiment; that if one advances confidently in the direction of his dreams, and endeavors to live the life which he has imagined, he will meet with a success unexpected in common hours.

Henry David Thoreau was born in 1817 in Concord Massachusetts. He was an author, teacher, naturalist and philosopher. We all have heard of his retreat to Walden's pond and the works he wrote there. The one above is from *Walden*, which was published in 1854.

Following our dream is something that we all have been taught early in life. It is the way to happiness and peace. That advice is still being taught, it's just that the dream has changed. Now it seems the dream is about something outside of me instead of my dream. Somehow the dream has been distorted; everyone must have the same dream of money, power, material grandeur, and social status. Someone else, not me, measures my success. I am only the mouse that follows the trail of the cheese. The cheese is not my flavor, but I follow anyway, in order to be called a mouse.

Imagination, as Thoreau points out, is a gift we develop within ourselves. It is created by thought and it is as diverse as we are. Imagination forms matter and becomes reality. It is what my world is built on, and gives me the energy to create. In a world of fast pace, fast facts, and fast talk, it's easy to forget what power lies within me. I get caught in the trap of deception, and wiggle to be set free.

So what's the answer, what's the cure, do I spend two years in the woods as Thoreau did, or do I stop and find myself? I find myself by dreaming my dream, then imagine I am living it, and let it manifest. My thoughts of success are different from yours, but that's OK, we all are connected and all of us contribute to the collective consciousness of love.

Being a spirit having a human experience, I can imagine I am so many things. I may imagine I am here to be of service to all life, and find happiness there. I may be a teacher, a farmer, a clerk, a priest, a homemaker and find peace. Whatever I think I am, I am. D.H. Lawrence put it this way:

This is what I believe:
That I am I
That my soul is a dark forest.
That my known self will never be more than a little clearing in the forest.
That gods, strange gods, come forth from the forest into the clearing of my known self and then go back.
That I must have the courage to let them come and go.
That I will never let mankind put anything over me, but that I will try always to recognize and submit to the gods in me and the gods in other men and women.
There is my creed.

Dreams and imagination are my tools, discernment is my guide and in Love, I co-create my life.

5. *Forever and Ever*

For nothing is fixed, forever and forever and forever, it is not fixed; the earth is always shifting, the light is always changing, the sea does not cease to grind down rock. The sea rises, the light fails, lovers cling to each other, and children cling to us. The moment we cease to hold each other, the moment we break faith with one another, the sea engulfs us and the light goes out.

James Baldwin was born in Harlem in 1915. He was a writer, storyteller and poet, who wrote about social and psychological issues that related to being black and homosexual. The question of identity is a focal point in his work. His statement above reflects his view of physical life. Nothing is fixed, everything changes, but the one constant is we are all connected, whether we remember it or not. I may be drowning in a sea in darkness, but I am still part of a collective consciousness. I am a whole part of another whole, which is a whole part of another whole—a holon, as Ken Wilbur describes us.

We are joined forever and ever in the stream of ALL THERE IS, Love. Baldwin's life was a lesson in learning about diversity. He teaches me that I am what you are. I may be another color, another race, or be of another religion or political thought, but I am what you are. The only thing that separates us is belief. Once I believe there is no separation, I accept, allow and respect all life. There is no segregation. There is only diversity and a clearer vision of why we are traveling through this physical journey.

James realized that this physical journey was not a journey of logic, but one of the heart—a journey of Divine expression. Feeling life with emotions and understanding there is so much I don't understand and hence, here I am. Here I am connected to all I experience. I want to express myself with my heart and become a grander version of myself. My belief is that we all know who we are. We are spirits connected in a web of consciousness that grows and expands as we do.

I can choose how to do that. I can do it by seeing love or fear in everything. Those are the choices. Love is reality; fear is an illusion. Love has no opposite when I realize it is ALL THERE IS. Love exists outside of linear time/space reality. It is the consciousness that fuels all other consciousness. The world of dualities is the world we create through the illusion of being separated from our source consciousness. This idea of separation creates fear.

Fear has opposites. Fear has many ways to manifest itself. Good and bad, right and wrong, hell and heaven live within this fear-based journey. When I face each day with fear I do nothing but create opposites.

Now is the moment to hold each other—to embrace our differences in love—to share unconditional universal service to all life.

6. *From My Heart and Eyes*

Love is a dormant state of awareness in most of us. It is a mysterious force that implants itself in the hearts and souls of humans. At conception, this mystery expresses itself through two people and at birth it becomes a physical being. Every child born in physical form is love manifested in pure expression. I don't think there is anyone who would dispute the fact that a newborn is the essence of love, formed by the seed of this great mystery that lives within us. I am like you—an example of that love. I am filled with it. It is a whole part of who I am and it never leaves me. However, I forget that fact as I travel through time, and view myself as someone who does not know what love is or how to find it. I search everywhere for this feeling of connection but I substitute other emotions to fill the void. Love is an elusive entity that I see and sense around me but can't find within me.

The foremost reason for dis-ease is not remembering who I am and not connecting to my source of power, which is love. I see myself as not worthy to be love or to experience it, so I create an illusion to live and hide in. I attract fear and suffer the effects of separation simply because I do not love this self in physical form. It's too big or small; too poor or wealthy; too ugly or beautiful; too sinful or hateful—all illusions of the duality I find myself experiencing because I believe that is my path in life and I must pay for the deeds of someone else. Little by little I destroy my physical form because I conform to the rituals of self-worthlessness. I don't love myself for that would be an act of conceit and egomania.

Actually it is quite the opposite; loving myself brings my ego in line with my emotions. I see everything and all life as extensions of my love as I offer it unconditionally. I am united with myself and express a zest for life that is filled with the energy of well-being. My eyes are the windows of my heart; they reflect the true nature of my soul—a reality filled with abundant peace. I create a world that sees the beauty in all life, even when it is dipped in contrast and trapped in fear. I express my gratitude through my words and deeds and light my path with remembering. I see my heart and enjoy the fruit of my seed.

Guiraut de Borneilh wrote a poem about love. Joseph Campbell notes it in his book, Creative Mythology. When I open my eyes and see the love I have in my heart, another me is born.

So, through the eyes love attains the heart:
For the eyes are the scouts of the heart,
And the eyes go reconnoitering
For what it would please the heart to possess.
And when they are in full accord
And firm, all three, in the one resolve,
At that time, perfect love is born
From what the eyes have made welcome to the heart.
Not otherwise can love either be born or have commencement
Then by this birth and commencement moved by inclination
By the grace and by command
Of these three, and from their pleasure,
Love is born, who with fair hope
Goes comforting her friends.
For as all true lovers
Know, love is perfect kindness,
Which is born- there is no doubt- from the heart and eyes.
The eyes make it blossom; the heart matures it;
Love, which is the fruit of their very seed.

Looking in the mirror, I see my eyes. I see my heart. I see my soul filled with ALL THERE IS, Love.

7. My Offering Is Peace. What's Yours?

If while you are presenting your offering to the altar, you remember your brother has a grievance against you, leave your offering there upon the altar and go and make peace with your brother. Then come back and present your offering.

Jesus, according to Matthew 5:23, is where you can find these words.

Pretty powerful message about how we deal with the emotions that cause anger, hatred, fear, and war in our world. I think he is saying resolve the conflict you have within yourself first, and then you will be able to resolve any ill feelings you harbor for others. Once that's achieved, you are connected to your God on the altar of love within you.

I don't know how many millions of people want peace; I know it is a great number. We all try in our own ways to bring about resolutions to conflicts that are currently in the news. Everyone has his own way of dealing with these issues, many pray, many fight, many pray and fight, some ignore it and others fuel it. No matter how you feel about it, your thoughts do affect what you focus on. If war is what I bring into my life, even though I'm against it, there it will be, I have attracted it. Whether I'm for or against it, the universe is giving me what I think about, war.

Each Sunday, churches are filled around the world, united in the belief that we don't want war. Each service has its own message on how to deal with the issue, and each person has his own belief about injustice. It may be that our collective consciousness is really fueling what we pray to resolve. By expecting the other side to relent and think my way, I am trying to control an action that restricts the universe from giving me what I want. My thoughts make resolution difficult unless I release myself and believe that peace already exists. That is my prayer and I see it in my mind, I live it and share it. I am not ignoring reality, for reality is peace. Which one do I want: war or peace?

Dwight Eisenhower said, "One day the people of the world will want peace so much that the governments are going to have to get out of their way and let them have it." We are our government, if our prayer is peace within ourselves, we will elect those who are peace loving, and that will be what we experience. There will always be contrast among diversity that is how we learn and grow. From those lessons we can present ourselves, as we are, connected to ALL THERE IS, in a web of love.

My offering Is Peace. What's yours?

8. Good Manners Anyone?

Good manners will often take people where neither money nor education will take them.

Fanny Jackson Coppin was born a slave in 1837 in Washington D.C. She went on to become the first African American principal of Philadelphia's Institute for Colored Youth which is now Cheney University of Pennsylvania. She traveled to South Africa doing missionary work with her husband Reverend Levi Coppin and they founded the Bethel Institute—a missionary school with self-help programs. In 1926, a Baltimore teacher training school was named the Fanny Jackson Coppin Normal School, which is now called Coppin State University. She lived a life of service performing everyday tasks with manners and dignity. Fanny Jackson Coppin day is held in Baltimore on April 15 celebrating the life of this gracious educator.

Good manners are vehicles I learned to ride early in my life. My parents taught me the value of manners and I experienced a wonderful flow of positive energy from everyone I came in contact with because of my words and action. During the first fifteen years of my life, I treated almost everyone with kindness, gentleness and grace. Then, something happened within me; my thoughts began to change and I no longer used the vehicles my parents trained me to use. I found a new tool of interaction called the ego and I began to focus on how I could get something from others without giving anything in return. I built a physical person around these thoughts and began to live my life using the goodwill of others to enhance my power. This pseudo power took me on a journey that was filled with pain, suffering and self-denial.

Through the years, I managed to use those old vehicles from time to time; and each time I did, they never failed me. I always got more than I gave and felt an inner sense of worth when I remembered how to live graciously. I found new friends and new opportunities in front of me waiting for me to experience them. Gradually, after years of narcissistic behavior and setbacks in my personal and business life, I began to repair those old vehicles. I realized that my journey through linear time is a school of learning. It is the awareness of each experience that keeps me alive in physical form. I can learn by being mannerly or I can learn guided by my ego which usually is a painful lesson. The choice is mine and I have done both. Both choices have gotten me where I am now.

Fanny's words are simple. They are easily understood, but hard to put into practice in this world of diversity. Being mannerly to the truck driver that has no consideration for road courtesy is difficult. The retail service worker who gives no service can be a painful experience. Then, there is the airline that is more concerned with revenue than the needs of their customers—that could be a nightmare as well. Situations like these are in my life so I can learn something about myself. Something I need to work on. It may be patience or understanding or it may be my manners. The lesson is something I forgot; I have always known what I need to learn.

Manners take me places that education and money can't take me. My spirit is filled with manners; they are an innate part of my being. Reconnecting to that innateness is a wonderful lesson. My life changes and I feel whole. I am thankful for every experience. I learn my lessons with dignity and grace. I accept my choices and live them in spirit.

Fanny, the teacher, is still teaching me and I appreciate her love. In spirit, good manners are the gifts I give everyone and they are the presents I receive in return.

9. Hope Has Feathers

Emily Dickinson is an example of hope and connection. Born in 1830, she wrote over 1,700 poems but only seven were published in her lifetime. The themes of her poetry are as large as her world was small, rarely leaving a bedroom in her father's home, in Amherst, Massachusetts. She did make short trips to Boston, Cambridge and Connecticut. She cherished the friends she had.

She wrote about fear, love, death, immortality and man's relationship to nature. She understood the meaning of being human and shared it with the world. She wanted nothing but the opportunity to express her spirit with poetic verse, and she did it in her unique style—a style that can be read, but not duplicated. Her work is one of a kind in its truth and vision. She reminds me that we are all unique in the way we express ourselves. Each of us brings a special quality to add to this physical world. We all make a deposit in the bank of wisdom, and we certainly make a lot of withdrawals. Understanding that my task is to be a connected branch on the tree of life is a noble deed. However many leaves, buds and flowers I produce is my creation. I get to perform my acts of living in the manner that suits my desire for expansion.

Emily found herself in a small corner of the United States in the nineteenth century, but she expanded her world to include all the centuries that followed her. Life after physical death is no myth for Miss Dickinson as she wrote:

Hope is the thing with feathers
That perches in the soul,
And sings the tune without the words,
And never stops at all,
And sweetest in the gale is heard;
And sore must be the storm

That could abash the little bird
That kept so many warm.
I've heard it in the chillest land.
And on the strangest sea;
Yet never, in extremity,
It asked a crumb of me.
(XXXII)

We never know how high we are
Till we are called to rise;
And then if we are true to plan,
Our statures touch the skies.
The heroism we recite
Would be a daily thing,
Did not ourselves the cubits warp
For fear to be a King.
(XCVII)

10. Fields Of Buttercups!

Could I but ride indefinite,
As doth the meadow-bee,
And visit only where I liked,
And no man visit me,

And flirt all day with buttercups,
And marry whom I may,
And dwell a little everywhere,
Or better run away

With no police to follow
Or chase me if I do,
Till I should jump peninsulas
To get away from you-

I said, but just to be a bee,
Upon a raft of air,
And row in nowhere all day long,
And anchor off the bar,-
What liberty! So captives deem
Who tight in dungeons are.

Emily Dickinson wrote that poem and marked it CII in her work
of *Collected Poems.* The beauty of her work is in its simplicity
of thought and natural imagination. To be a bee and flirt with
buttercups is the pure music of thought, and it dances through
the air of unity with grace as its partner. Emily put the puzzle of
life together by watching nature live in the now.

The message of unity is all around me. All I need to find it
is awareness. If I can stop for a moment and sense the magic
of nature, my problems would dissolve in the honey of
consciousness. I can be a bee and dwell a little everywhere if

256

I allow my thoughts to take me there. I am already connected to the energy that flows through all life and I can tap into it anytime I choose; when I believe and then become.

What liberty it is to realize that I can row in nowhere all day long and still be all I desire. There are no dungeons unless I create them. I'm the only one that locks my self in a cell of fear. The bee has no fear; it only has a now filled with the buzz of happiness.

Now where did I put my wings? Spring is here and blossoms are dressed for marriage. The nectar of oneness drips into my thoughts and I am free to jump from reality to reality filling my world with love. The essence of my spirit is anchored off the coast of eternity, where fields of buttercups whisper my name.

11. Love Diet

A body is forsaken when it becomes a source of pain and humiliation instead of pleasure and pride. Under these conditions the person refuses to accept or identify with his body. He turns against it.

Fritz Perls was a German psychiatrist and one of the founders of Gestalt Therapy in the twentieth century. Gestalt therapy is concerned with the nature and structure of what we perceive in the present moment. How I think about myself now affects my world of events. As Kierkegaard said, "Life is not a problem to be solved, but a reality to be experienced."

Perls' statement about my forsaken body is worth remembering. Rather than feeling angry and confused about how I look, and disconnecting from that pain, I should accept and understand it as my creation, not the work of food, drink or marketing. I choose to fuel myself in many ways. I perceive how I want to live now, and from those choices I become the physical form I live within. Instead of cursing myself for over indulgence, forgiveness would be the road to acceptance. I can look at myself and see the "me" I want to be, and begin living it. Of course, in acceptance I realize that change is a tool to help me see myself with loving eyes. Changing my thoughts about who I am changes my appearance.

It's all about love and remembering that reaching for a better thought about myself is worth more than the superficial gestures I give myself and others. Those gestures put a temporary cover over the real issue.

Self-love comes before everything else. Not ego love, but the love that is innately within me—the love that is connected to all life in a Divine Matrix of Love. In remembering that connection,

I am who I am and everything I want to be. I see myself in
the physical form that feels good to me. Whatever form it may
be, it's mine and I love it. I free myself from the illusions of
someone else fixing a problem that I created by my thoughts.
That freedom is the remedy I need to see the real me who loves
all life, starting with my own.

Nothing changes in this reality unless I believe it. Then, I
can experience it. Then, I can express and share it. My world
becomes that change and I appreciate it.

Big or small, round or flat, I am what I think, and if I love that
thought, I've created my diet—a diet that works all the time.

12. With Each Breath

No pessimist ever discovered the secrets of the stars, or sailed to an uncharted land, or opened a new heaven to human spirit.

Helen Keller was born in Alabama in 1880. She was the first deaf and blind person to graduate from college. She was an American author, activist, and lecturer who became a campaigner for workers' rights and an advocate for many progressive causes. Helen taught through example and her legacy is timeless. Her words above describe her feelings about vibrations. I can be a pessimist and live in pain, or I can vibrate in sync with my inner self and discover a world called heaven.

Through the years, I have experienced the agony of pessimism. I used external remedies to cure my mental ailments. I functioned in a haze where everyone and everything were pawns to be used and abused in order for me to feel better. My thoughts told me I was in an unloving world and I had to become something other than what I was in order to be recognized. I fooled my friends and family and I functioned as an empty shell that was filled with nothing but self-hatred. Drugs and alcohol ruled my behavior and I became the victim I perceived myself to be. I wrestled with frustration, anxiety, and pity and soon found myself in a room of fear with no doors or windows. I was trapped. My world got smaller and my life became a nightmare.

One day the room exploded and my life changed drastically. The lie that I lived was exposed; I was filled with shame and loneliness. Guilt ran through my body and I finally asked for help. I asked my source of energy to free me from the hell I found myself living in. I asked for forgiveness from those I used, abused, and hurt. I forgave myself for my self-centered egotistical pessimism, and I opened myself to the universe around me. I let the power of universal optimism flow through my body, and I now accept myself for what I am. Finally, I can allow myself the freedom to express my feelings honestly.

Change is growth; change is happening constantly in this world of magic. I am a changeable spirit in human form. I am on a mission of discovery, finding my truth first, and then living in its gentle love of pure awareness. In my truth, I find new beliefs and open new doors that contain rooms of miracles and myths. I can be whatever I want to be and live graciously in unity with all life. I share the zest of new ideas with conviction and follow my path to the stars in gratitude.

Helen was right; pessimism brings me nothing but more of what I have. Vibrating in sync with my inner truth brings me all I'll ever need. Abundance, peace, and opportunity abound in free will—my free will to choose from the infinite probabilities that surround me. I know who I am now, and I change freely and optimistically with each breath I take.

Journey

1. A Choice of Consciousness

What you regard to be senility is the gradual relinquishing of the present and the desire to be gone from this place and time. This signifies the loosening of the ties between consciousness and body and the consciousness spending more and more time out of the body to experience adventures of another kind.

Jani King wrote those words in her book, "The Gift." Senility is not the destruction of a life but the transition to another state of being. That is not how I look at the onset of old age, but then I have been taught to look at things as black or white; right or wrong; good or bad. I only see what I think I see, so my vision is directly related to my thoughts. Aging is the deterioration of my physical and mental state and I no longer serve a purpose if I believe that life is for the young and old age is a waiting room for death. Our society is based on external appearances and material possessions; therefore, when I hit a certain earth age my worth as a human is somewhat compromised. Life is filled with yesterdays and the hint of a new tomorrow.

Jani explains senility as a conscious desire to be somewhere else. It is my choice to move from one state of being into another whenever I want to change. I do this when dreaming and when I daydream; I take myself to another place through my thoughts and enjoy the experience of another reality. My thoughts create my world and they continue to do so while I am in my physical body, regardless of age. Age is a state of reference; a guide to lead me into discovering other aspects of myself. This tool of physical life can be used to enhance my awareness or it can be my sentence of finality. The choice is mine.

The state of growing older is a gift; it opens new roads to travel on my journey and new adventures to experience and express. My consciousness begins to blend within itself and I feel comfortable with who I am. My senses expand to enjoy the life forms that exist around me. I am filled with gratitude and appreciation for all I have and all I have been. Beauty is in everything and I live in acceptance and peace. Innate knowledge comes forth in each moment and I live for today. Filled with the energy of light, I resist nothing and allow my spirit to speak in unity.

Senility is a choice I make to move to another place. It is not the road everyone chooses but it is a way to remove myself from pain and suffering before I die. I can be senile or I can live in old age fully aware of my body, mind, and spirit. There is no right or wrong in my choice. Each is a vehicle for growth; the question is how do I want to fully become the spirit I am and when do I do it? The road is long and filled with choices and the probabilities that surface from my choices create what I experience. Senility is freedom and a choice of consciousness.

2. A Creature of the Now

Listen to the salutation to the dawn,
Look to this day for it is life, the very life of life.
In its brief course lie all the verities and realities of our existence.
The bliss of growth, the splendor of beauty,
For yesterday is but a dream and tomorrow is only a vision,
But today well spent makes every yesterday a dream of happiness
And every tomorrow a vision of hope.
Look well therefore to this day
Such is the salutation to the dawn.

This Sanskrit greeting to a new day is full of wisdom. It tells me to live in the now, there is only now, filled with unpredictable events that become reality in my world. I choose to experience many probabilities in this day and make them matter by my thoughts. I reach into a well of knowledge and express my physical being in creativity. My waking dream is one of expansion and learning. I become a grander version of the "I" that I imagine I am.

Today is filled with love, happiness and joy if I allow those feelings to exist. That is my choice. Through the contrast of daily life, I am able to see myself in a mirror of change and adjust my tempo, so I can accept each new challenge and grow from it.

A new dawn is a new world, a new reality that I create in order to remember who I am. Filled with energy from my Source, I give that energy to everyone I meet today. My consciousness flows in the river of wellness and it touches everything in harmony. That is the essence of my journey today.

I am a new song waiting to be heard. I am a new joy waiting to be expressed. I am a new dawn waiting to be light. I am a new love waiting to be kissed. Today, I am I—a creature of the now.

3. A Dried up Puddle of Problems

There is no such thing as a problem without a gift for you in its hands. You seek problems because you need their gifts.

Richard Bach, born in 1936, wrote the book *Jonathan Livingston Seagul* as well as several other works. The quote above is from Illusions: *The Adventures of a Reluctant Messiah* published in 1977. Problems always have gifts attached to them, but I sometimes get so trapped in the problem, I overlook the gift and wallow in my own pit of frustration.

Every act I perform is a problem if I think it is. I only see the roadblock and never see the road. I second-guess my worthiness and myself; my life is a village of pain and I see nothing but anguish. Each day I fight and battle these problems wanting to win; to be the giant that kills the flea. It's me against them in a raging war of my own thoughts. The fleas win and the giant in me becomes another flea feasting in a world of self-pity.

Words are the road maps I use to travel on my journey. How I label my destination creates that destination. These labels become my experiences and then my expressions, followed by me becoming the label I created. I can use any word I want to describe a thought; it is my choice to name what I create. No one else needs to be present for me to manifest that thought.

A roadblock could be a sign of trouble or it can be a blessing. That sign is simply how I perceive it and how I experience it. We all see the same, but think differently; that is the gift of diversity.

How I react to the diversity that surrounds me is a matter of choice. It can be a gift that I open and use to expand and grow; or it can be a problem that swallows my mind and fills it with fear. Choices create my road and that path is my own construction.

Life is filled with free choices and the road to awareness is an open mind; a mind that expresses a willingness to face diversity and accept it as the gift of growth, expansion and the expression of my Source.

In Jonathan Livingston Seagull, Bach says, *"The trick, according to Chiang, was for Jonathan to stop seeing himself as trapped inside a limited body that had a forty-two-inch wingspan and a performance that could be plotted on a chart. The trick was to know that his true nature lived, as perfect as an unwritten number, everywhere at once across space and time."*

My trick is to know my true nature; to know that all the situations I call problems are created by me in order to remember who I am. That trick changes my perceptions; it changes my choices and brings me the gifts of connection, awareness and unity. In each so-called problem is a spark of unity that lights my path of remembering. I light that spark with thoughts of gratitude and acceptance. And, the fire that results is a flame of oneness that lights my world with ALL THERE IS, Love.

I soar across my sky of dreams, my spirit has wings, the gift of diversity is looking up at me and smiling in a dried up puddle of problems.

4. A Puff in My Sky

Shinkichi Takahashi was born in 1901 in Japan. He is considered one of Japan's great master Zen poets. He received the Ministry of Education Award in 1973 for his collected poems known as *Triumph of the Sparrow*. His expression of philosophical insights is as important in his work, as emptiness is in Zen. No matter how you view the world of Zen, Takahashi's imagination has a dizzying power. It is a cosmic trip through space and time, traveling past this reality and settling in a universal consciousness that is connected to all realities.

I found some of his work translated by Lucien Stryk and would like to share it.

Shell

Nothing at all is born,
dies, the shell says again and again
from the depth of hollowness
Its body
swept off by tide—so what?
It sleeps
in sand, drying in sunlight,
bathing
in moonlight. Nothing to do
with sea
or anything else. Over
and over
it vanishes with the wave

Cloud

I'm cheerful, whatever happens,
a puff in the sky—
what splendor exists, I'm there.

Moon and Hare

Things exist alone.
Up on the moon
I spot Hare
in a crater
pounding rice to cakes
I ask for one.
"What shape?" says Hare.
"One like a rocket."
"Here—take off!"
Up and out,
pass everything
at once,
free at last—
unaware of
where I'm heading.

Gods

Gods are everywhere:
war between Koshi and Izumo
tribes still rages.
The all of all, the One
ends distinctions.
The three thousand worlds
are in that plum blossom.
The smell is God.

Shinkichi boarded his rice rocket in 1987 and is traveling around the universe, now aware of where he is heading. Like the shell, he is never born nor does he die. Instead, he travels through the waves of my consciousness like the smell of God. A puff in my sky!

5. I Am the Future

You are the future,
the red sky before sunrise
over the fields of time.

You are the cock's crow when night is done,
You are the dew and the bells of matins,
maiden, stranger, mother, death.

You create yourself in ever-changing shapes
that rise from the stuff of our days --
unsung, unmourned, undescribed,
like a forest we never knew.

You are the deep innerness of all things,
the last word that can never be spoken.
To each of us you reveal yourself differently:
to the ship as coastline, to the shore as a ship.

Rainer Maria Rilke, the master poet of Modernism in the
German speaking world, was born in 1875. He was born and
raised in Prague, but spent most of his life traveling across Europe.
Rilke is the poet's poet; his mastery is unsurpassed and his
craftsmanship is exceptional. The poem above describes the
inner voyage he traveled throughout his physical life. He realized
that my connection and awareness of a greater self was mine
to discover in my own way. Each one of us connects to other
aspects of our consciousness with a different style. Some take
the road of religion, others take the path of nature, and others
search within themselves and live as reclusive souls. Rilke knew
that all I have to do is look around me to find the heaven I seek.

Thoughts of red skies, sunsets, and a forest filled with life all possess and express my desire. Right before my eyes, no matter where I look, I see a grander version of expression. Every petal, stem, and root is filled with the consciousness of being. The cow, pig, horse, and buffalo graze in a field of awareness. Mountains, valleys, oceans and deserts speak in tongues of connection. The stars and planets glow with energy and Mother Earth changes with expansion. All are there for my benefit; to teach and guide me on my journey. It is my choice to feel the love that surrounds me. My free will sets the stage for happiness or for suffering.

Rainer got the message. He understood the puzzle. He wrote about his freedom so I could share his knowledge. Rilke and I are not separated by time. He lives on this page with me. His words are as fresh today as they were the day he wrote them. Consciousness has no expiration date. It has no judgment or fear. It expresses itself in love and beauty, and I am a whole part of it.

No matter what path I travel in my journey of remembering, I will reach my future. It is where Rilke is. It is the place I never left. I am the future.

6. A Sage or Ordinary Man

*When an ordinary man attains knowledge, he is a sage; when a
sage attains understanding, he is an ordinary man.*

I found this Zen proverb this morning and it hit me that knowledge
is one thing and understanding is another. Both provide insights
and probabilities on my physical journey. I am always seeking
knowledge and then I try to understand what I have learned.
Sometimes I find what I call knowledge, as it sits quietly within
me, waiting for me to wake it from its sleep. I discover that I
have the ability to understand that my innate sense of being
is filled with wisdom, but have forgotten that fact. So I try to
awaken myself by understanding that I AM.

Enlightenment is understanding; it is not a religion or a
new thought of salvation. There is nothing to be saved from
but myself. Enlightenment is the awakening of knowledge and
understanding that brings me to a place of peace. Each path of
discovery is different. Each one filled with the feeling of living.
My path may be different from yours but it doesn't matter for
we all get to the same place—the place we never left. The place
of knowledge and understanding that makes us ordinary in a
non-ordinary way. It is the place where the sage in me meets the
ordinary man I am, and I reconnect to ALL THERE IS, with
the awareness of my freedom. I live connected to all life and
feel the abundance of love that surrounds me. I become one with
nature, with the universe, and I enjoy the opportunity to express
myself in physical form. I begin to live an ordinary life in a
non-ordinary way.

So, the proverb does hit a nerve within me; the nerve of
remembering that I am here to learn and grow into a grander
version of who I am—a spirit having a human experience.

7. A World of Snores

There ain't no way to find out why a snorer can't hear himself snore.

Samuel Clemens, better known as Mark Twain, looked at life with wit and satire and it brought him fame and popularity. His novels, essays and quotes live in the minds of people around the globe. They are timeless, priceless and thought provoking. Why does the snorer not hear himself snore?

I'm sure that question could be answered in many different ways, depending on who I ask. The doctor has one reply, the pastor has another, and the snorer has his own way of answering, by not listening. It's not that he doesn't want to listen; he is too busy doing something else to bother himself with why he's doing it.

Allowing is the best cure for curiosity. Sooner or later the answers arrive. In fact, the more we allow, the more things come. They come from that place where the snorer goes when he needs relief; relief from all the questions; relief from all the confusion of everyday life; a safe place filled with the power of healing; the power of knowing and the power of unity; a haven for the weak, the homeless and the mighty. Every one of us goes there and connects with another aspect of our consciousness.

Snoring is the noise that my body makes when it is on autopilot. It is the sound of inter-space travel from one level of consciousness to another. As my wife can tell you, I have been to the outer boundaries of the universe based on the turbulence I create while sleeping. I never hear a thing, nor do I remember my journeys within myself. I don't realize my abilities to interact with non-physical matter, I was never taught to think that way. In fact, I was taught not to think that way.

I wake ready to face another day, with more contrast and more growth, not remembering the trip I took to the far reaches of my psyche the night before. I create a new day, but fail to understand that my nightly journey is the foundation for my waking creations. I do remember some things; strange episodes with people, places and things that confuse my mind. I see myself in different situations, fearful encounters and sorted experiences. There are old friends, relatives and associates speaking to me in foreign languages. A world of mystery surrounds me as I snore my way to unknown, but known, places. Half of my physical life is dedicated to this travel in awareness. My physical awareness is enhanced because of these trips.

The snorer never hears himself snore, but knows he is on an adventure. An adventure in consciousness where there are answers to all the questions; where there is unlimited love and appreciation; where there is unity without form and life in tranquility. That is the place I came from and now I realize I never left behind. It is the world of the snorer!

8. Double Vision? How about Quadruple Vision?

*Now I a fourfold vision see, and a fourfold vision is given to me.
'Tis fourfold in my supreme delight and threefold in soft Beulah's
night and twofold always. May God us keep from single vision
and Newton's sleep.*

William Blake is describing feelings and senses in this work
titled "Fourfold." He is mentioning Newton's sleep, which
explains that consciousness sees only the external world,
the material world of Newtonian physics. Soft Beulah's
night refers to the state of poetic inspiration, the poet's muse.
Blake describes his delight in being able to have an all-inclusive
vision of understanding, which is thinking, feeling, sensation,
and intuition.

Blake certainly had visions that were foreign to many who read
his work in the eighteenth century, but as we know today, his
thoughts were ahead of his times. I think we all feel that there
is more to us than just physical form, although in daily life
that's all we focus on. The challenge is to see ourselves for who
we really are. It took me years to understand that my thoughts,
emotions, feelings and intuition all work together to make my world.
I create the day-to-day experiences. I need no help to be angry
or hateful—I do that all by myself. I can also be loving, peaceful,
and giving with no help from anyone. In fact, that is my natural
state of being if I allow it.

The trick is to practice what I know, and to not over react to
situations that look foreign to me. Just by taking the time to
think before I speak, I can make my life much better. By seeing
all the contrasts I encounter as opportunities for learning helps
me face and get through each uneasy event. Asking for help

from the Source of my energy, and see it manifested is the greatest tool I own. It works all the time. It may not happen exactly when I think I want it, but it does come once I release myself and believe.

My external world is a mirror for my internal feelings. Understanding that makes me feel my way through life instead of just observing and reacting to physical things and seeing them as the work of another person or thing. It takes practice and patience. Someone once said, "The reward for patience is patience." I believe that.

Blake was on a journey of discovery over 200 years ago. We are on that same journey today. How we travel is our choice. My choice is to be who I am, to look within myself, and to feel my emotions and let them guide my way. I choose to love my higher self, my Source of energy, and stay connected to it. My well-being is my freedom. It's a gift to share with all life.

9. *Faster than the Speed of Light*

Last night I asked an old wise man to tell me the secrets of the universe. He murmured slowly in my ear, "This cannot be told, only learned.

Rumi's words in the book, *Crazy as We Are*, translated by Dr. Nevit O. Ergin, are true. No one else can tell me about the universe that is within me. It reaches places I know, but have forgotten. Its secret is just a thought away.

Quantum physics is revealing a new approach to learning. It is explaining that everything I experience has its inception within me. Thoughts create the matter I see around me. They create the events I live, and dreams are the workplace where the events take shape. All that time while I'm in bed and snoring is actually productive use of my consciousness. I also get to feel what it's like to live without the restrictions of time and space. Now, that's learning!

It seems we are each our own universe, within another universe that is comprised of many universes. As Rumi said, this cannot be told, only learned. I have the knowledge to understand this new way of thinking within me, but it takes a new approach for me to accept it. No one can do it for me; I have to experience it myself. My beliefs must change in order to learn. It's like Newton opening himself to the ideas of quantum physics, or Einstein realizing that there are things that travel faster than the speed of light. As Einstein pointed out, I must solve secrets by thinking differently than the thoughts that created the secrets.

In order to crack the mysteries of the universe, I need to look within myself and resolve my own mystery first. I must realize who and what I am before I can express what I want to share. By using my feelings I can search within for answers. I can

278

begin to unravel the knots of distortion that have covered my thoughts. I can free myself from the outside influences that have controlled my life. It only takes a thought to make that so. Then, I must think it enough to make it a belief. By mining within myself and uncovering my truth, I release trapped energy that has been destroying the body that supports me. I can be and do so many positive things if I believe in myself and in my universe.

Rumi knew this over 700 years ago, and he is still teaching me to learn about myself. If I understand the most important lesson, "know thyself," my universe is no longer a secret. It is a magnificent wonderland filled with ALL THERE IS.

10. What is Real?

"What is real?" Asked the Rabbit one day, when they were lying side by side... "Does it mean having things that buzz inside you and a stick-out-handle?"

"Real isn't how you're made," said the Skin Horse. "It's a thing that happens to you. When a child loves you for a long, long time, not just to play with, but REALLY loves you, then you become real.

"Does it hurt?" said the Rabbit.

"Sometimes," said the Skin Horse, for he was always truthful. "When you are real, you don't mind being hurt."

"Does it happen all at once, like being wound up," he said, "or bit by bit?"

"It doesn't happen all at once," said the Skin Horse. "You become. It takes a long time. That's why it doesn't often happen to people who break easily, or have sharp edges, or who have to be carefully kept. Generally, by the time you are real, most of your hair has been loved off, and your eyes drop out and you get loose in the joints and very shabby. But, these things don't matter at all, because once you are Real you can't be ugly, except to people who don't understand."

Margery Williams was born in London in 1881. She wrote children's books. The Velveteen Rabbit was her most famous work. She had the innate ability to use inanimate objects and animals to express human feelings and emotions. The above excerpt shows the beauty of her work. She writes from a child's perspective and is truly inspirational in her art.

Being real is something we all want to be. I want to live in reality; I have been taught to do that over the years. As I travel through time, I wonder what that word means. It seems there are many realities to live, all of them waiting for me to experience them. But, being real is something else. It is what I am or become when I know myself. There can be many realities, but my being real is unique to me. Margery tells me it's not about my physical appearance or what address I have. It's about becoming. It's about love. It's about awareness and connection. It's about freedom. Somewhere between birth and death in linear time I become real; we all do.

For some it is immediate knowing and continues to grow and blossom through time. For others the road is filled with pain, agony and suffering before the real self becomes alive. It all is a matter of choice. How I learn to be me is my work and I create it. Once I know who I am: ugly or fat, rich or poor, young or old, nothing else matters. I can share and give myself in gratitude, just as the Velveteen Rabbit did. I feel love within me and around me and offer my service in unconditional unity. As the Skin Horse said, once you're real you can't be anything but All There Is, love.

11. The Tooth Fairy and Santa

Physicists Albert Einstein and Richard Tolman showed that if quantum mechanics describes events, then even the past is as uncertain as the future. So how do we have any past at all? The answer is that we create them! Yes. What we call the past only exists in the windmills of our mind. We in the present are responsible for our pasts, not the other way around. We are the creators of history.

Fred Alan Wolf, the physicist who appeared in the movie, *What the Bleep Do We Know"* can really stir the pot of thoughts within me. His words above are hard to swallow at first, based on what I have been taught over the years. At one point, I thought there really was a tooth fairy and a Santa Claus. Then, I discovered they were not real. Other people were acting out these myths, but I believed them and I got what I asked for. So, in my reality, there is a tooth fairy and a Santa in my now. I got what I wanted by believing and expressing my thoughts. I do create my past in my now.

The idea that I can change my past is a difficult one to accept using my current method of thinking. I must reinvent the way I look at my life. Ideas of linear time and space based on my focused conscious perceptions are just one part of the self I call me. In order to awaken different aspects of myself, I must allow them to surface freely and then begin to accept them. These other aspects of consciousness are there and I experience them all the time; I just don't realize I am because I have trained myself to block them as unwanted experiences. I am living many lives simultaneously, but I only focus on one through the illusion of linear time.

Okay, I know this is not the typical understanding of life. But, what if it is true? What if I do believe it? Just like the tooth fairy and the round man in the red suit, it becomes what I call real. My world becomes an open field of possibilities—a vast universe of perceptions and choices that I have hidden from myself because I focused on just one reality. Consciousness creates thoughts. Thoughts create matter. Matter contains the consciousness of my thoughts. With that in mind, I can change my past as well as my future, now.

12. The River of Time

Becoming time is not difficult. It's like entering a flowing stream and allowing ourselves to drift along with it. As we flow with the river, the water that appeared to be rushing past when we stood upon the shore suddenly becomes quiet and motionless. It's the same when we enter the river of thought. We lose time simply because we become it.

Fred Alan Wolf, the quantum physicist, teacher, author, and media personality, tells us a lot about who we are in the above statement. I can see time as something to fear, or I can unite with it by understanding who I am. When I think about it, I realize that part of my consciousness flows in time, just as my physical body flows in the river. I become time to experience it, not to be controlled by it. It is a tool of remembering, not a weapon of destruction. Of course it's hard to see anything but the effects that time takes on my physical body, so I learn to fear and dread time as my mortal enemy. Time causes death and I want to live forever.

Fred is telling me that my thoughts change my viewpoint of time. I need not be separated from it, or scared of it, but I can blend with it and understand how it works.

It is common knowledge that time slows down the faster we travel. At the speed of light it stops and there is no time. My consciousness is not controlled by time, because it is faster than the speed of light. It was there before my birth and it will be there after my physical death. So, I am experiencing time with just one aspect of my consciousness. By slowing down a part of myself, I become aware and focused on time in order to grow and learn. The universe is not a part of time, but I think it is, just as I think I am a part of time. Actually another me is pure consciousness expressing in many different ways, blended in a web of ALL THERE IS, Love.

In order to understand time, I need to think about who I am. Not only as the physical body and the watch that sits on my arm, but the consciousness that chose to experience the illusion of time. Knowing that it is my choice to experience the wonders of time, I can unite with it and enjoy it. Time is not a villain, but a teacher pushing me to express another aspect of myself.

My time is your time. Age does not exist in unity. Love is the only time, and it never stops.

TM

Wholeness

1. A Child in a Week

A child in a week
Becomes a week smarter
A child in a week
Learns fifty new words
A child in a week
Can bring change to himself
An adult in a week
Is the same as before
An adult in a week
Turns over the same weekly
An adult takes a week
Merely to scold a child

Shuntaro Tanikawa was born in Tokyo in 1931. He writes poetry, children books, and scripts for television and radio. He has translated into Japanese the cartoon Peanuts and the text of Mother Goose. His works are popular throughout Japan. Kids in primary and secondary school memorize his poetry and learn about living in the world of free verse and rhythms.

Tanikawa's work above tells me something about what I have become as I traveled from childhood into the adult stage of my life. It is almost like I left my innate knowledge locked in a vault, and discovered another form of learning. This new form of learning restricts, hinders, and controls my ability to remember who I am. I become another self who thinks in terms of ego satisfaction and fights the world I find myself living in. Everything becomes a struggle and each day seems to hold the sameness of yesterday, and the sadness of tomorrow. My existence has no meaning and my memories have no life. Caught in this adult world of suffering, I wander from drug to drug, pain to pain, trying to find the vault I left behind.

A child in a week becomes a week smarter. I become a week weaker and race towards old age and disease with the hopes that my agony will end quickly. Consciously I don't show it, but all I have to do is look in the mirror to see the creature I have created. The child looks in the mirror and sees the love that surrounds her. The adult looks at the child and sees the dreams that he left behind. Lost in adulthood, I exist in the world of misguided thoughts and emotions.

The interesting thing about this path of remembering is the contrast I encounter. I experience it to learn and grow into a grander version of myself. Remembering the child within me, brings new energy to my thoughts—the thoughts that create my world.

What I believe, I experience; what I experience, I express; what I express, I become. If I want to be that child who uses his innate wisdom to learn and grow, all I need to do is think that way. I can still be an adult and dream like a child. In fact, dreams do not discriminate; they are the foundation for reality at any age.

I can be the adult who learns fifty new words this week, the adult who becomes a little smarter this week, the adult who finds his vault of love and opens it with awareness—the awareness of my connection to a web of consciousness that is essence of all life. In spirit, I have no age. I am the child and the adult simultaneously. I express and expand with the energy of pure love. That love never leaves me. I am a whole part of the wholeness of infinity.

I know that time measures my physical existence. I can use that time to be the child who knows no fear, anger, hatred or war. I can be the child who dreams of magic kingdoms and mystical journeys. I can be whatever I think. That is the world I live in.

2. A Little Soul Searching?

There is a soul inside your soul. Search for that soul. There is a jewel in the mountain of being, look for the mine of that jewel. Search inside if you can, not outside.

Rumi, the thirteenth century theologian and teacher, lived in Turkey. He was born in Afghanistan, and he dedicated his life to writing about unity—the unity of man to man, man to God, religion to religion, and man to himself. He continues to spread unity 700 years after his death, through his vast writings, which have been translated into English within the last 70 years. He lived by the law of attraction. He didn't call it that, he just lived it.

He understood that he was a jewel, and he spent his life mining the mountain within himself, so we all could find the mountain of jewels that rests within each of us. As he pointed out, there is a soul within our soul, and it's time to rediscover it.

Words, especially words translated from another language, sometimes lose their original meaning. We see it in all the ancient texts we have studied over the years. There is always a different way of explaining those words depending on what each of us thinks and believes. I may think the words mean something completely different from another who reads the same thing. The wonders of diversity are always at work, and it is okay for me to believe what makes me feel good. No need to agree.

I have found the mountain of jewels within myself. It's my mountain and as I look around the world, I see many different mountains displaying their own special beauty and character. I think we all are different jewels from a connected mountain range.

Education has told me about the soul, but I never heard about a soul within a soul explained that way. It does make sense. I am a soul, and God is a soul, so I must be the soul within His soul manifested physically. That would mean I have been looking for Him in the wrong place. Not up or down, or in a specific place, He is within me, in fact, is me. That would mean that God is the soul within every soul and that everything is God. We are connected to a universal mountain of jewels that shines outwardly to express love and compassion and expand in gratitude.

My quest in physical form is to polish my jewels; to shine with the brilliance of a new star; to create a necklace of unity that contains the jewels from all life, and to share that wealth in peace and abundance. I am what I think. I am a soul within a soul mining myself to become the grander version of who I am. Shining in the reflection of all life is unconditional universal service at its best.

3. Am I Forgetting Something?

Everybody forgets something. My keys, my glasses and my notes to remember not to forget all seem to vanish before my eyes. I search and find them with a bit of frustration and go on my way. Then, I think, "Why am I so forgetful? Why am I so unfocused?" Well, in the rush to accomplish the simple tasks of daily life, I only focus on one thing at a time unless I remind myself to broaden that focus. Every little act is a lesson in awareness. Every tiny thought is an opportunity for connection.

Acceptance is an act of freedom. Forgiveness is an act of love—especially when I forgive myself. Focusing on the love within gives me the strength to change. It gives me the power to remember who I am. That brings me to a place of peace and I begin to see life for what it is, the path of remembering and the journey of discovery. I discover a grander version of myself and begin to live in that awareness.

I found this poem about forgetting, and it hit me that my forgetfulness is the catalyst for change once I focus on it. The poem was written by the U.N. Environmental Sabbath Program, and I found it in the book *Earth Prayers from around the World* edited by Elizabeth Roberts and Elias Amidon.

We Have Forgotten Who We Are

We have forgotten who we are
We have alienated ourselves from the unfolding of the cosmos
We have become estranged from the movements of the earth
We have turned our backs on the cycle of life

We have forgotten who we are
We have sought only our own security
We have exploited simply for our own ends

We have distorted our knowledge
We have abused our power

We have forgotten who we are
Now the land is barren
And the waters are poisoned
And the air is polluted

We have forgotten who we are
Now the forests are dying
And the creatures are disappearing
And humans are despairing

We have forgotten who we are

We ask forgiveness
We ask for the gift of remembering
We ask for the strength to change

We have forgotten who we are

This message of remembering teaches me that I have the ability to make a difference in the world around me. All I need is to focus on what I know and to remember who I am. Forgetting my keys is the bell that reminds me to remember that I am connected to all life in the web of consciousness that brings me back to the place I never left.

4. Am I Young Enough?

I'm not young enough to know everything.

Sir James Mathew Barrie was a Scottish novelist and dramatist born in 1860. He is best known for his work, Peter Pan, the boy who never grew up. Sir James is also credited with the creation of the name "Wendy," which was non-existent in Britain or America before he gave it to the heroine of Peter Pan. The first stage performance of the play was in 1904 and Barrie gave the copyright of the play to a leading children's hospital in London.

The magic story Barrie created is one that most children learn about early in physical life. I remember my first encounter with Peter and his band of children and the glorious Tinkerbell faithfully guiding their journeys. I became immersed in the idea that this notion of freedom the kids were living was real and I could live my life the same way. My imagination took over and off I went on adventures that took me to places and introduced me to people I never knew. Briefly, I lived in a world made up by my thoughts and enjoyed the freedom of wakefully dreaming. Those episodes were as real to me as my mother's call for me to come home for dinner.

I learned that I could be anything I wanted to be by imaging that I was the person or thing that excited my emotions. My youthful life was filled with the energy of my thoughts and I lived in several worlds simultaneously and functioned normally—or at least I thought I did. I went on missions of mercy and flights of triumph in order to express my zest for living. I became the hero that overcame the shadows that appeared in physical life. My feats of grandeur were performed anywhere. All I needed was within my mind. I could disappear from any arena that inhibited my enjoyment simply by using my thoughts and youthful ignorance.

I grew up and found myself conforming to the rules of
manmade laws. Daydreaming was out and certainly thinking
that I was something other than a mind and physical body
was a no-no. I was taught that there was only one reality
and everything else was nonsense including my childhood
adventures into other worlds. I became a rigid, selfless form of
matter that had to comply with the acts of sameness that locked
me in a container of someone else's opinions and judgments.
I was brainwashed by the system that professes to be reality.
I had been split in two and I lost my ability to feel whole.
I functioned in a society that took a dim view on experiences
that could not be explained rationally by manmade laws of
science and religion. I could not know everything, for I was
tinned by age and misguided by fear. Life is a mystery only to
be discovered at death and any variation of that fact is heresy, so
they said.

Sir James was correct I'm not young enough to know everything;
I don't allow myself that freedom. I think in linear fashion and
express myself in numbers rather than thoughts. I allow my
body to weaken and crack by the stress of separation and I invite
dis-ease into my experience to punish myself for my loneliness.
I seek help from everyone, but help no one in return. I measure
my success by my possessions rather than by my dreams. I pray
to a God that I fear. I expect to be punished for my beliefs. I wait
for death, but fight its arrival. I question my creations and use
anger and hatred to hide from my truth.

I'm not young enough to know everything I am—unless I
change my thoughts. I can relive my youth and be whole in
my dreams. My imagination creates my experiences and my
impulses guide me through my emotions. Letting go of my
fears by accepting them and releasing them, changes this old

me and the world around me. I can be free by using the energy within me to create wellness. I can be anything and everything by reconnecting to the source of ALL THERE IS, Love. I am always a youth in spirit and I am forever grateful for the physical opportunity to express my true self.

5. An Eruption of Emotions

*An eruption of emotion is characteristic of the spontaneous
shift of an idea from the level of sentiments to that of sensual
consciousness. Furthermore, the appearance of such an eruption
obviously means that a certain spiritual process has reached a
conclusion. The observation of the process escapes the test of
conscious thought, since it enters consciousness only after or at
the moment of completion. However, inasmuch as the idea is, it
must have become. The process is creative in the highest sense
of the word. The phase of becoming takes place on the level of
the sentiments, while that of being is on the conscious plane.*

Leo Frobenius was born in Berlin, Germany in 1873. He was an
archaeologist and a major figure in German Ethnography. He taught
at the University of Frankfurt where the school's institute of
ethnology was named after him in 1946.

Leo's statement correctly describes how my emotions work.
There is an impetus that projects a thought into a conscious
action that I manifest. My emotions give me the feeling of
being in this time/space reality, and I judge them as right or
wrong, good or bad, depending on my environment. The idea
could be a simple one, but how I think about it with my focused
consciousness can alter it drastically. I can make a mountain a
valley, or an uplifting thought a nightmare. My emotions take me
on a physical journey of heaven or hell, depending on my beliefs.

As Frobenius points out, the impetus that creates the physical
action is spiritual. My life consists of many consciousnesses
although I focus on this present journey with only one aspect
of it. My emotions are the language of spirit there to interpret
the messages given by other aspects of myself. They guide me
through this physical journey and protect me from the human
ego I have developed.

When my emotions are allowed to function from within, my physical life becomes a spiritual one as well. I am able to connect with the sentiments that Frobenius talks about. I become aware of a greater energy that expresses itself through me. I expand and grow from the emotion of ALL THERE IS, Love.

I am a human being on this plane of existence, but that is just one part of who I am. I am connected to all life in the web of the Divine Matrix, which is the source of all consciousness. The vastness of this web reaches infinity and back again. With that thought in mind, I am never alone. I have the power within me to be the change I want to feel. Within me, is a world of uncharted beauty waiting to be remembered. Within me is the freedom to love myself, and share that love in unconditional service to all life.

I am being human on this conscious plane, but it's only a small part of the sentiments that thrive within me.

6. An Untangled Web

The spider, dropping down from the twig,
Unwinds a thread of her devising:
A thin, premeditated rig
To use in rising.

And all the journey down through space,
In cool descent, and loyal-hearted,
She builds a ladder to the place
From which she started.

Thus I, gone forth, as spiders do,
In spider's web a truth discerning,
Attach one silken strand to you
For my returning.

E.B. White was born in Mount Vernon, New York in 1899. He was an essayist, author, humorist, poet and Pulitzer Prize winner. He wrote the children's books now considered American classics: Charlotte's Web, Stuart Little, and the Trumpet of the Swan.

The spider, as White points out in the above poem, lives in a connected web. That's not a new revelation, but the way that White looks at the spider is.

For many years I was afraid of these creatures. There was always at least one around, no matter where I went. How and why it got there was a mystery. My task was to destroy it and its web. I was taught that it would hurt me or even kill me, so I would be the aggressor and reclaim the space I called mine.

Certainly that method of dealing with unwanted or fearful things was a learned experience. I didn't come into being with the thoughts of destruction; I only had thoughts of connection, thoughts of unity, and thoughts of love.

E. B. explains how I am very much like the spider, weaving a web of thoughts around the world I live in. They can be thoughts of enjoyment, caring and trust, or they can be thoughts of fear. Each thought catches another thought and my web is gradually built into a world of matter. I then travel through my web experiencing all the matter my thoughts have trapped. This journey can be one of profound joy or a trip of pain. I absorb whatever is in my web and live my life accordingly. I make my web my heaven or hell, always changing and growing as I experience my creations.

My physical web is a metaphor for the web that I have always been connected to. I am part of a universal web of consciousness that is constantly spinning and expanding as I do. E.B. realized his connection by keeping one silver strand of thought attached to the universal web. That strand is the awareness that everything is one. My web is a whole part of another whole, all joined in the infinite web of ALL THERE IS. By spinning my web with thoughts of love, gratitude and sharing, I expand into a grander version of the spider in White's poem. I remember why I am creating my web and feel the love that it becomes. I experience all life the same way. I express my thoughts in compassion and understanding. I release my judgment and accept discernment.

As White says, I spin my way back to my beginning, the place where I started, which is the place I never left; I only thought I did.

7. Body Intelligence

The word "connection" is a plural one; a connection involves more than one thing. The word "awareness" is the same way. I have to be cognizant of something else in order to be aware. I use those two words a lot when I write. It seems that I am in one sense a word, but there are many words to describe me and what makes me who I am. Certainly, I can use "connected awareness," to describe me. After all, there are many things I am connected to and many things I am aware of. I am plural in a singular form, but I don't see myself that way most of the time. I go through each day thinking that there is only one me to deal with the challenges that face me. I forget that I am connected and I can always be aware of that connection, if I allow myself that luxury.

My friend, Rumi, lived over 700 years ago. He knew about connection and awareness. He saw himself as more than a Turkish villager who worked hard and experienced the pain of living in the Middle Ages. He wrote about the life he experienced, and he used his connection to pull himself (and those who read his work) out of the daily feeling of separation and into the connected awareness of a higher self. In simple understandable words he described the thoughts of the people, and explained that in simplicity there was a greater good; a greater whole that fills the emptiness within them. He taught them to feel that worth and be a plural being living in single form.

I found his poem "Body Intelligence" in his book *The Essential Rumi* translated by Coleman Barks and thought the message was worth writing on this page now. As you can see, Rumi may have lived in physical form many years ago, but his spirit is here, helping me demonstrate connected awareness and spread its meaning.

Body Intelligence

*Your intelligence is always with you, overseeing your body, even
though you may not be aware of its work.*

*If you start doing something against your health, your
intelligence will eventually scold you.*

*If it hadn't been so lovingly close by, and so constantly
monitoring, how could it rebuke?*

*You and your intelligence are like the beauty and the precision of
an astrolabe.*

Together, you calculate how near existence is to the sun!

Your intelligence is marvelously intimate.

It's not in front of you or behind, or to the left or the right.

*Now try, my friend, to describe how near is the creator of
your intellect!*

Intellectual searching will not find the way to that king!

The movement of your finger is not separate from your finger.

*You go to sleep or you die, and there's no intelligent motion.
Then, you wake and your fingers fill with meanings
Now consider the jewel-lights in your eyes.*

*How do they work? This visible universe has many weathers
and variations.*

But uncle, O uncle, the universe of the creation-word, the divine command to Be, that universe of qualities is beyond any pointing to.

More intelligent than intellect and more spiritual than spirit.

No being is unconnected to that reality, and that connection cannot be said. There, there's no separation and no return.

There are guides who can show you the way.

Use them. But, they will not satisfy your longing.

Keep wanting that connection with all your pulsating energy.

The throbbing vein will take you further than any thinking.

The prophet said, "Don't theorize about essence!" All speculations are just more layers of covering.

Human beings love coverings!

They think the designs on the curtains are what's being concealed.

Observe the wonders as they occur around you.

Don't claim them. Feel the artistry moving through, and be silent.

Or say, "I cannot praise You as You should be praised. Such words are infinitely beyond my understanding."

8. *Bridge of Love*

Steven Longfellow Fiske is an award-winning singer/songwriter, poet and advocate for peace. His book, *The Art of Peace, A Personal Manual on Peacemaking and Creativity*, is in its second printing.

Peace. I fight so hard to get it. I kill, hate and destroy all in the name of peace, but I do show compassion for what I destroy? I give comfort to the soldiers and families I sent to fight in the name of peace. Then, I bury them with tears of remorse.

I build resentment for those whose beliefs are foreign to me and my government punishes them with embargoes, threats, and war. Freedom is my cry of salvation and I battle with my own sense of justice in order to obtain it. My freedom is locked in thoughts of retribution with nothing but a gun and the vision of a merciful God.

The law of attraction explains how the universe works. The more resistance I feel about something and the more I push against it, the more of it I attract into my life. By fighting for peace I bring more fighting in my world, not peace. Nothing is ever achieved by destruction. I live in a world of creativity where I vibrate with positive energy and the peace I want already exists. The only action I need to take is to let it flow through me and allow the peace to be who I am.

Fiske wrote a song called, "Bridges of Love," that tells how a bridge can bring me the peace I seek.

Bridges of Love

If we can build great bridges
Across the mighty waves, between the distant ridges
Is it a task too great
To build a bridge across the depths of hate?

For now more than ever
What the world needs more of
Is to reach for each other
With bridges of love

If we can reach so far
To send men up to the moon and rockets to the stars
Why are we still so far apart?
Why can't we find the way from soul to soul,
From heart to heart?

For now more than ever
What the world needs more of
Is to reach for each other
With bridges of love

Bridges of steel reach from shore to shore
Bridges of love reach so much more
They link our common hopes, our common ground
Joining one and all, the whole world round

We all can build bridges of love each day
With our eyes, our smiles, our touch
With our will to find a way
There is no distance we cannot span
The vision is in our hearts
The power is in our hands

What the world needs more of
Is to reach for each other For now more than ever

With bridges of love

A simple bridge can change my world. A bridge of oneness and awareness connects all life. My task is to know that I am peace. I am love. I am you. My path is to remember who I am, and allow my focused consciousness to unite with the stream of love that flows through my bridge and into everything.

9. Champagne Anyone?

Kilgore Trout once wrote a short story which was a dialogue between two pieces of yeast. They were discussing the possible purposes of life as they ate sugar and suffocated in their own excrement. Because of their limited intelligence, they never came close to guessing that they were making champagne.

Kurt Vonnegut was an American novelist born in 1922. He wrote several novels: *Slaughter House-Five, Cat Cradle, and Breakfast of Champions.* His words from *Breakfast of Champions* above are very true indeed. Like the yeast, I do have a hard time realizing what I am creating in the daily act of survival. At times, it seems that I am suffocating in my own waste and I feel that my life is without purpose. I fall in the pit of self-pity and try to pull everything around me in the pit with me. I trap myself in a world of negativity by my thoughts.

Just like the yeast, I limit myself with these thoughts of unworthiness. In reality, I am creating a purpose-filled life. I may stumble and trip along the way, but my journey of remembering is filled with miracles. Each moment of each day brings more opportunities. If I focus on what someone else has achieved or accumulated, I take my abilities for granted because in my mind they do not measure up to the standard of excellence I perceive around me. I am too busy looking at the outside world to realize what is taking place in the world within me.

I do create my life through my thoughts. I can be whatever I believe I am. There are many probabilities presenting themselves to me in my waking hours, as well as my dream state. I choose from those perceptions and live them. I can vibrate with positive energy by thinking that way and always feeling what my emotions express. When I ask for help from my source, it always appears; all I need to do is feel it. I become the champagne of life by knowing who I am from the start. At some point I forgot that fact, but now is the time to reconnect to who I really am.

In every thought a form of matter is created. I can pick my creations and live them abundantly. I co-create my experiences with my fellow spirits, and we can design a world of peace, joy and love by our choices. We can feel the energy of nature and reconnect to it. We can see a world of diversity and live in harmony with it. By being aware that we are not alone, we can love each other in spite of the contrast that our physical journey creates. We are one in the champagne glass of life, bubbling with the effervescence of ALL THERE IS, Love, and enjoying every sip.

10. I Will Meet You There

Constantine Cavafy was born in 1863 and is considered one of the Mediterranean's greatest poets. He was born in Alexandria and lived there most of his 70 years. I found one of his most well known works again this morning and wanted to share it.

"Ithaca" was written in 1911, and describes the value of appreciating our journey, rather than always rushing for the destination. It describes living in the now, and what it means to have no fear, for our thoughts create our daily monsters. It explains that now can be filled with happiness and abundance, if we believe it is, and it can be as long or as short as we make it, our prayers lead the way.

We all are on the road to Ithaca, how and when we get there is our choice. Cavafy describes the path to awareness and what it means to travel the road of discovery within ourselves.
It is a work that is timeless, priceless and real. I'll meet you there!

Ithaca

When you start on your journey to Ithaca,
Then pray that the road is long, full of adventure, full of knowledge,
Do not fear the Lestrygonians and the Cyclopes and the
angry Poseidon.
You will never meet such as these on your path,
If your thoughts remain lofty,
if a fine emotion touches your body and spirit.
You will never meet the Lestrygonians, the Cyclopes and the
fierce Poseidon,
If you do not carry them within your soul,
If your soul does not raise them up before you.
Then pray that the road is long.

That the summer mornings are many,
That you will enter ports seen for the first time with such
pleasure, with such joy!
Stop at Phoenician markets, and purchase fine merchandise,
Mother of pearl and corals, amber and ebony, and pleasurable
perfumes of all kinds,
Visit hosts of Egyptian cities, to learn from those who have
knowledge.
Always keep Ithaca fixed in your mind.
To arrive there is your ultimate goal.
But do not hurry the voyage at all.
It is better to let it last for long years;
And even to anchor at the isle when you are old,
Rich with all that you have gained on the way,
Not expecting that Ithaca will offer you riches.
Ithaca has given you the beautiful voyage.
Without her you would never have taken the road.
But she has nothing more to give you.
And if you find her poor, Ithaca has not defrauded you.
With the great wisdom you have gained,
With so much experience,
You must surely have understood by then
What Ithacas mean.

11. How Sweet the Lilt

*How am I to contain my spirit lest it touch on yours? How lift
it through a space higher than you to things environing? Oh, I
should gladly lay it by to rest in darkness with some long
forgotten thing at some outlandish unresounding place which
won't re-echo your deep echoing. But all that touches you and
me comes so, it takes us jointly like a stroking bow that draws
one voice from two strings by its tilt. Upon what instrument then
are we strung? And by the hands of what musician wrung?
Ah sweet the lilt.*

On my journey through poetry I found many special people.
They lived at different times, in different countries, and spoke
different languages. Their physical lives were diverse. Some worked
to make a living, all lived to make music—the music of poetry,
the rhymes of unity, the lilts of freedom. A connected swing of
oneness that is always present and captivating.

Rainer Maria Rilke is one of those people. He opened my eyes to
so many things that are right in front of me. In his poem, "Love
Song" (above), he shares profound wisdom. My spirit has been
resting in darkness in some unresounding place with no echo.
How and why I put it there is another story—the story of fear,
distortion and greed. I walk in a haze of guilt, waiting to find my
spirit, and play my precious instrument—the instrument that is
strung with the strings of love.

Just the thought of finding what I had hidden for some many
years, brings it knocking on my memory. I can't hold it in that
dark place when I realize I put it there. It joins me without
conditions and reveals a world that I turned my thoughts away

from in order to satisfy my ego. Reunited within, my internal music begins to play. I speak and echo the thoughts of my source. I am the stroking bow of one voice. I am the sweet lilt of gracefulness and gratitude. I am nature dressed in flowers, birds covered in feathers, fish filled with plankton.

There is no separation in the music of love; its rhythm swings from every branch and tree. Its value is my awareness, connection, and freedom to express it and expand in its creation.

12. *Shadow Clings to Form*

Everything is based on mind, is led by mind, and is fashioned by mind. If you speak and act with a polluted mind, suffering will follow you, as the wheels of the ox cart follow the footsteps of the ox. Everything is based on mind, is led by mind, is fashioned by mind. If you speak and act with a pure mind, happiness will follow you, as a shadow clings to a form.

Siddhartha Gautama was born in Nepal around 410BC or 563 BCE. His father was King of the Shakya nation, one of several ancient tribes in India. He was a prince with three palaces for seasonal occupation, meaning they used them at different times each year.

The king shielded the prince from religion and the suffering that existed around the country. At 16, the prince was married at a wedding arranged by his father. Soon, he had a son named Rahula. Siddhartha was provided with all the material wealth he wanted. However, wealth was not his ultimate goal.

After spending 29 years as a prince in Nepal, Siddhartha left the palace in order to meet his subjects. His father tried to hide the sick, suffering, poor and homeless people from his sight but it was not possible. The prince saw diseased people and decaying corpses. He was depressed by such great suffering and by what he encountered on each trip away from the palace. He was so moved by these events, he escaped from the palace and began the life of an ascetic and begged for alms in the streets. He found two hermit teachers that guided him in meditation. He totally deprived himself of worldly goods including food. He nearly died of starvation. After going through these experiences he found what is known as the middle way, a path of moderation, away from the extremes of self-indulgence and self-mortification.

He meditated for 49 days and at the age of 35 he attained enlightenment. From that day on he was known as the Buddha, or awakened one. His awakening was his insight into nature and he realized that human suffering is caused by ignorance.

He began teaching what are known as the four noble truths:

1. We all experience suffering in one way or another: mental, physical, emotional, spiritual.

2. We create our own suffering. It is a consequence of our desiring things to be some way other than they are.

3. It need not be this way. We have a choice as to how we perceive the world and live our lives.

4. There are systematic ways to go about changing how we think and perceive.

Siddhartha lived 2,400 years ago, but his words are as fresh as a newborn baby. His life was dedicated to living in the now and experiencing both the human and the spirit that co-existed within his mind. His words bring me to a place of peace, a restful place of awareness.

Just like the followers of Jesus, Siddhartha's followers began a religion based on his teachings. I wonder if Jesus knew of the teachings of this man from India. Where did Jesus travel in those years of his life that remain a mystery? The messages of Jesus sound familiar, and are similar to those of Siddhartha. There certainly was trade and communication going on between these two regions. After Jesus died, Thomas made a trip to India and established a Christian community that is still thriving today.

Regardless of that, the message that our thoughts create our world and our reality has been taught for centuries. I can live without suffering if I choose that belief. I can reconnect to my spirit in my own way; I don't need anyone or anything to do it for me. I can perceive myself to be an expression of my Source and grow through my love and service.

As Buddha said, everything is based on the mind, is led by
the mind, and is fashioned by the mind. I am what I perceive
myself to be. Just like Jesus and Buddha I can be enlightened by
reconnecting to nature and to all life through my thoughts of unity.

The human images of Buddha and Jesus are long gone, but
their shadows still stand right in front of me. Their message
of freedom fills me with love and gratitude. Their shadows of
abundance cling to my form.

......Presume not that I am the thing I was;
For God doth know,
So shall the world perceive
That I have turn'd away my former self......

~Shakespeare

One More Thought

One In Diversity!

Giovanni di Bernardone was born in Italy in 1181. His mother was from France and wanted her son to become a great religious leader like John the Baptist. His father, Pietro, was in France on business when Giovanni was born. When he returned to Assisi he was furious with his wife and refused to allow his son to become a man of the church. Pietro renamed the boy Francesco in honor of his mother's heritage. Francis spent most of his youth lost in books. He had no desire to enter his father's business and in 1201 joined a military expedition against Perugia where he was captured and held prisoner for a year. Francis returned to Assisi and had several life-changing experiences. He started to care for lepers and began begging at church doors for the poor.

He spent a lot of time alone asking God for enlightenment. At a church outside of Assisi, he had a mystical experience where an icon of Christ crucified came alive and said to him three times, "Francis, Francis, go and repair My house. As you can see, it is falling in ruins." Francis thought this meant the ruined church where he was praying, so he sold his horse and clothes and spent time with the parish priest repairing the church of San Damiano.

This was the start of St. Francis of Assisi's life. He later founded the Franciscan order devoting his life to poverty and caring for animals and the environment. He wrote many wonderful messages, but the one that I have in my journal is this one:

Lord, make me an instrument of your peace.
Where there is hatred, let me sow love.
Where there is injury, let me sow pardon.
Where there is doubt, let me sow faith.
Where there is despair, let me sow hope.

Where there is sadness, let me sow joy.
O Divine Master, grant that
I may not so much seek
To be consoled as to console,
To be understood as to understand,
To be loved as to love.
For it is in giving that we receive.
It is in pardoning that we are pardoned.
It is in dying that we are born
to eternal life.

Those words say so much, yet are so simple. It is a path of understanding—a path of forgiveness. It is the way of love, the voice of spirit uniting us in the stream of ALL THERE IS.

St. Francis' words inspired me to write a poem called "Simultaneously" that has been published by several newsletters and websites. It is part of my 2007 Collection. My thoughts compliment the words of St. Francis. They are expressed in gratitude and universal service. I share them now to connect with the essence of being one in diversity.

Simultaneously

I Create God In My World
With Gentleness and Gratitude
With Loving Acts Of Kindness
With Warm Words Of Giving
With Forgiving Bands Of Friendship
With A Joyous Heart Of Oneness
With Abundant Rings Of Mercy
With Overflowing Respect For All Life
With Connected Awareness
Of Being
With Self Love Knowing That
I Am His Likeness

I Am His Vision
I Am His Actions
I Am His Thoughts
I Am His Spirit
I Am His Peace
I Am
So That I May Be Like Him
I Am
So All Can Be Like Her
I Create God
As He Created Me
Simultaneously

Acknowledgments

Grateful acknowledgement is made to the following for permission to reprint material copyrighted or controlled by them.

Earth Prayers from Around the World: Harper San Francisco

The Gift Jani King: Light Source Publishing

Robert Fulghum, *Words I Wish I Wrote*: HarperCollins Publishers

The Little Zen Companion: Workman Publishing-New York

Waking up in Time: Origin Press Inc.

Act of Faith Conversations with P'taah: Light Source Publishing

Life Styles of the Rich in Spirit: Hay House Publishing

Integral Psychology by Ken Wilbur: Shambhala Publications, Inc.

Emily Dickinson Collected Poems: Barnes & Nobles Books

The Soul's Code By James Hillman

Today's Gifts Daily Meditations for Families: Halzelden Foundation

Love And Friendship edited by Jane Parker Resnick: Longmeadow Press

Tao Te Ching by Stephen Mitchell: Harper Perennial

Rumi We Are Three, translation by Coleman Barks: Maypop Books

The Glance Rumi Translated by Coleman Barks: Penguin Putnam Inc.

The Poetry of John Paul II Roman Triptych: USCCB Publishing

Dr. Quantum's Little Book of Big Ideas by Fred Alan Wolf: Moment Point Press Inc.

The Parents Tao Te Ching by William Martin: Marlowe and Company, New York

Psychic Politics, Jane Roberts: Moment Point Press

Crazy As We Are Selected Rubais from Divan-I Kebir: Hohm Press

The Zen Doctrine of No-Mind, D.T.Suzuki: Samuel Wiser Inc.

The Unknown Reality, Jane Roberts: Amber-Allen Publishing, Inc.

The Nature of the Psyche, Its Human Expression: Amber-Allen Publishing, Inc.

The Individual and the Nature of Mass Events, Jane Roberts: Amber-Allen Publishing, Inc

The Essential Rumi: Translated by Coleman Barks: HarperCollins Publishers

Winters' Tales Stories and Observations for the Unusual by Jonathan Winters: Random House, Inc.

Leaves of Grass: David S. Reynolds: Oxford University Press

The Book of Runes: Ralph H. Blum: St Martin's Press

The Path of Self- Transformation: Eva Pierrakos: Bantam Books

Agartha: Journey to the Stars: Meredith Young-Sowers: Stillpoint Publishing

Contact Page

For more information or to purchase another copy of this book,
visit **www.shortsleeves.net** or email **hal@shortsleeves.net**

Snail Mail:
Short Sleeves Insights
1013 Chapel Ct.
Franklin, Tennessee 37069

Other Books by Hal Manogue:

Short Sleeves A Book For Friends 2006 Collection
ISBN 0-9778130-0-2

Short Sleeves A Book For Friends 2007 Collection
ISBN 0-977-8130-1-0

Short Sleeves A Book For Friends 2008 Collection
ISBN 0-977-8130-2-9

About the Author

Howard (Hal) Thomas Manogue, was born in Philadelphia, and is a forerunner to the Indigo children, a now age term for misfit with an intuitive nature, a desire to know his truth with a gift of giving and sharing. Hal retired from the shoe industry after 35 years of sole searching, and discovered his real soul.

He enjoys art, music, philosophy, psychology, nature and people.

His poems have been published by: Mystic Pop Magazine, Children Of The New Earth Magazine, New Age Tribune, Seasons Of The Soul Newsletters, Lightship News and Writers In The Sky Newsletters. His essays can be found on **www.ezinearticles.com, www.authorsden.com, www.faceyourself.com, www.ascension.net, www.selfgrowth**. com and 0ver 500 sites other around the world. Hal's Blog and Website: **http://halmanogue.blogspot.com/ www.shortsleeves.net**

He lives in Franklin Tennessee.

Printed in the United States
203098BV00002B/106-129/P

9 780977 813032